DON'T LET *Dementia* STEAL EVERYTHING

AVOID MISTAKES, SAVE MONEY, AND TAKE CONTROL

Kerry Peck and Rick L. Law

AMERICAN BAR ASSOCIATION
Senior Lawyers
Division

Cover design by Shawn Hunt/Relevant Designs

Printed in the United States of America.

22 21 20 19 18   5 4 3 2

Library of Congress Cataloging-in-Publication Data
Names: Peck, Kerry, author. | Law, Rick L., author.
Title: Don't let dementia steal everything: avoid mistakes, save money, and take control/ By Kerry Peck and Rick Law.
Description: Chicago : American Bar Association, 2018.
Identifiers: LCCN 2018015137 | ISBN 9781641052030 (print)
Subjects: LCSH: Dementia—Patients—Legal status, laws, etc.—United States | Practice of law—United States.
Classification: LCC KF3803.D46 P43 2018 | DDC 362.1968/3100973—dc23
LC record available at https://lccn.loc.gov/2018015137

Discounts are available for books ordered in bulk. Special consideration is given to state bars, CLE programs, and other bar-related organizations. Inquire at Book Publishing, ABA Publishing, American Bar Association, 321 N. Clark Street, Chicago, Illinois 60654-7598.

www.ShopABA.org

TABLE OF CONTENTS

Chapter 10
Stop the Money Thieves! Scammers, Opportunists, and Family Members

PREFACE

Expert View: I Have Become My Wife's Parent

Dr. Dean Bryson has a PhD in educational psychology from the University of Nebraska. During his professional career, he has worked with numerous individuals, primarily in the family setting, but also dealing with crisis situations involving hostage taking. In addition, he has worked in cross-cultural relationships with the Sioux Nation. One of his proudest moments is having been inducted into the Sioux tribe and given a Sioux name.

Q: Dr. Bryson, give me some information about yourself and your qualifications to speak to attorneys about dealing with elderly people.

A: Last July, I turned 75, and I'm married to a 75-year-old. I started working with elderly people when I was in graduate school at the University of Nebraska in 1963, and I've been working with them ever since. I've lived in senior citizen centers; I've lived in dementia centers; I've lived in assisted-living centers. And my wife with dementia is living in a rehab center and will soon go into a dementia center.

Q: Could you tell me about your journey with your wife? Could you explain a little about what it means to be a psychologist married to a person with Alzheimer's?

A: I first became a parent to my wife eight years ago. That's when I first started noticing changes; perhaps it's an occupational hazard of being a psychologist. We know that the loss of short-term memory is the single most common symptom of any form of dementia—and there are many forms of dementia. 50 percent of them will be Alzheimer's-type and the other 50 percent will be spread among the other types.

For us, it was the little things. She started to develop aphasia—looking for the right word. She was a teacher and she started to stumble—wanting to say something, but the right word wouldn't come. We've all done that, but in normal forgetting, it will come back in a few minutes, or in an hour. But with my wife and so many others, it doesn't come back. What so many people do is try to reason with the person with dementia and say, "Just relax. Take a couple of minutes." To try to reason with someone who is losing the ability to reason is pointless. It isn't going to happen.

Then it became forgetting more and more common, everyday activities. She loved to cook, but now was forgetting many of her recipes. Then it got to not answering the phone, then to not knowing how to use the phone. And then it progressed to forgetting how to read, then forgetting how to write. . . . Then it progressed to forgetting how to eat, how to bathe, and how to take medications. And then the wandering began, which is very common. So there were times when at night—and I typically go to bed around midnight and get up around five—that within the five hours that I tried to sleep, I would be up as many as 16 times with her, night after night.

That became too much after a while. I put alarms on every door so that if she opened the door, the alarm went off, but it got to the point where there was just no way I could take care of her and keep her safe. She was a threat to herself, whether it was wandering or it was something in the house. So we sold everything—our house and everything—and moved to a facility where I could live in the independent living area and she could live in the Alzheimer's unit and be taken care of 24 hours a day. So now she's in a facility and she needs help with everything—dressing, brushing her teeth, combing her hair. Physically, she's still incredibly healthy. She's still fully ambulatory. No other illnesses, no other diseases, no disabilities.

Q: That gives us the perspective of what you've gone through.

A: A lot of times, people with dementia will just sit and look at you and not talk. They want *you* to indicate what they need to say. Or they'll say, "I know what I want to say, but I just can't find the words." Or they might not even call their son or daughter by their right name.

I love elderly people. There's no other way I can say that. They're sometimes frustrating, but so am I. They are sometimes confused, but so am I. I love them. They are a challenge.

FOREWORD

Scott Turow

In my 2013 novel, *Identical,* Tim Brodie, an elderly private investigator, who hopes to unravel the mysteries of a murder that took place nearly three decades before, visits a nursing home so he can interview Lidia Gianis, 87, a woman Tim has known for years, but who is now deeply in the grip of dementia:

> "Is he my husband?" Lidia asked Eloise, her attendant, as Tim entered.
>
> "Oh no, honey. He just a friend." Eloise propped Lidia up in the leatherette recliner. "You all go head and visit. I'm just outside, case you need me."
>
> Tim sat down in a wooden-armed chair a few feet from Lidia.
>
> "Do I know you?" she asked Tim.
>
> "Tim Brodie, Lidia. We met a million years ago at St. D's."
>
> "I don't know you," she said. "I had a stroke and my memory is not so good."
>
> "Yeah, well, my memory isn't what it once was either. "
>
> In thirty years on the police force, and twenty-five since then as a P.I., Tim had done lots of interviews under daunting circumstances, questioning children and the mentally handicapped, and naturally enough, the desperately bereaved. But this would be a new chapter and Tim had no idea how to start.

On Lidia's bedside table, there were photographs of her two daughters and of her twin sons and a passel of kids.

"Now who are all these folks?" he asked her.

"I don't know. The girl just put them there. But they're all nice people."

Tim picked up one photograph, a group shot of Lidia's grandchildren.

"Now these grandkids of yours, they're a good-looking bunch." Tim meant it. The Gianises were always a handsome family.

Lidia was frowning. "Is that who they are?" she asked.

"Beautiful," Tim said, "All of them."

"Yes, I think they're all nice people. I have a son, did you know that?"

"Two, I believe." He tapped the picture beside her of her identical boys.

"My sons come here all the time. One of them is a big deal, too. Is he an actor?" she asked Tim, referring to Paul who was now running for Mayor. "People just love him. They tell me so all the time. Everyone here knows who he is."

Tim said he knew Paul too, then asked about Cass, hoping for any information about the other twin.

Lidia pondered a second and shook her head. "I had a stroke and my memory's not so good." She raised her hand again to stare at her bracelet, which, by whatever logic was left to her, once more brought her attention to Tim. "Who are you?" she asked. "Do I know you?"

This dialogue, unfortunately, is based more on experience than imagination. My mother, who passed in 2011 at the age of 91, spent her last six years increasingly confused by dementia. The perseveration and repetitions that characterize Lidia's conversation became familiar to me, as did the fact that my mom could have unpredictable flashes of amazing lucidity. Caring for her was always a challenge, even though I had the complete support of my sister, Vicki, who shared the responsibility with me, and the heroic assistance of two wonderful cousins, Joy and Sy Dordick, who spent time with my mom, and often stood in for me when I was travelling. Nonetheless, when my mom lay dying, I felt compelled to ask her whether she wanted to go on with her life. That was simply not a decision any of us felt we could make for her.

"Are you ready to quit?" I asked my mother.

She shook her head no. I doubt that she understood the full implications of the question, but she got the basic point and Alzheimer's or not, my sister and I abided by her decision that she was not ready to die. The medical interventions continued, although she was gone days later, notwithstanding.

The complexity of that moment and of entrusting such a profound question to someone whose capacities were so compromised makes for intense family drama. But the legal implications of such situations are in many ways even more difficult to unravel.

That is why this is such a fascinating and important book. It is not the usual ponderous legal treatise. It's a practical quick-start guide so that you can be a beacon to a family member, a friend, a loved one, or even a co-worker who has been affected by the darkness of dementia.

When it comes to understanding Alzheimer's disease, every one of us knows someone who has been affected but the disease is so pervasive and frightening that many of us try to block it from our minds. When someone asks us what they should do now that a loved one has been diagnosed, we don't even know how to begin to find the right answers. This book will be your starting point and a trustworthy guide. It is written by practicing lawyers who are on the front lines fighting to serve clients with Alzheimer's disease and their families. In this book they share with you their secret wisdom, and the uncommon knowledge that comes from years of multiple client experiences.

You are about to meet some great storytellers and many deeply admirable people. The authors know that no matter how well attorneys fulfill their legal role, when it comes to Alzheimer's disease, dementia sufferers and their families need help from a team of capable and concerned professionals. Within these pages you will hear from nurses, legal guardians, advocates for elder-abuse victims, hospice personnel, Alzheimer's Association leaders, technology visionaries, geriatric psychiatrists, police officers specializing in scam prevention, family caregivers, forensic experts, and even prosecutors. Each one has an important story to tell that will provide you with the gift of deeper understanding.

Alzheimer's disease is one of the scourges of our time, and one whose toll on the country will only deepen with the aging of the Baby Boomers and the inevitability of increased life spans. Curing Alzheimer's would probably do more than any single step to reduce health care expenses and, far more important, improve the quality of life of the elderly here and around the world. But until there is a cure, you'll be grateful to have this book at your side.

INTRODUCTION

Why You Need This Book

When dealing with Alzheimer's disease, most families don't even think about the law as it applies to their situation. Unfortunately, it is a standard legal truth that *everyone* is presumed to know the law. That's right, *you* supposedly already know the legal traps within Medicaid nursing home care governmental benefits; legal penalties caused by receiving gifts from a person with Alzheimer's; and legal obstacles to preventing a loved one from continuing to make disastrous financial decisions.

This book's authors and publisher, the American Bar Association, want to help you to avoid making big and expensive mistakes. This book can help you take the right first steps to understand the issues raised by a diagnosis of Alzheimer's disease.

This book is designed to be used by the reader as a reference guide to finding quality legal advice to overcome some very common legal obstacles. Chapter 1 is designed to be an overview and a guide as to where to find specific information within the other chapters. Each chapter is designed to stand on its own.

In our experience, something has happened that is motivating you to need help and you would like to obtain that help as quickly as possible. First, read Chapter 1 and the table of contents. Second, jump to the chapter that seems to address your current painful concern. Third, read some of the other chapters—they are designed to provide you with information that you don't know that you need to know.

We have **bolded** certain legal terms or other terms that we feel that non-lawyers are less likely to be familiar with throughout the book. These terms are included in a glossary at the end of this book.

We, the authors, Kerry Peck and Rick Law, are attorneys who focus on the issues of aging. Both of us are referred to as "elder law attorneys." Nonetheless, we each concentrate in different aspects of the law of aging (elder law). Kerry Peck is the lead partner of Peck Ritchey (www.peck-bloom.com) and Rick L. Law is the lead partner of Law Elder Law (www.lawelderlaw.com).

Mr. Peck is a nationally famous Chicago trial attorney focused on estate, elder law, and trust litigation. He has seen the worst of what can happen when people take advantage of a loved one or other vulnerable person with wealth.

Mr. Law is a nationally known elder law estate planner who spends almost all of his time working with clients within his office. His legal practice involves meeting with clients and their families and then creating the paperwork necessary to provide them with valuable solutions in the areas of estate planning; retirement income tax and long-term care asset protection.

In this book, the authors write in the first person and referred to themselves corporately as "we."

This book is not meant to provide specific legal advice to you. We can provide only general legal advice. Long-term care issues and governmental benefits must be dealt with under state and federal law. You are encouraged to use this book as first aid and as a first step, and then to contact experienced and capable legal counsel in the state of residence of the loved one with the long-term care concern.

CHAPTER 1

DIAGNOSED WITH ALZHEIMER'S DISEASE: WHAT ARE WE GOING TO DO?

"Bob has been diagnosed with Alzheimer's disease! What are we going to do? Am I going to lose my home? Are we going to lose everything?"

The caller was a dear friend, Luise, a woman in her 60s whose husband, Bob, was 72 years old. She was the organist at her church and taught children to play piano. Bob was a Korean War veteran and a retired policeman. With Bob's diagnosis, they lost their hope of a comfortable retirement of enjoying their long and fulfilling marriage. Only one of them had been diagnosed with Alzheimer's disease, but they both were victims.

Bob was a former amateur chess champion, so he was well aware that he was mentally declining. He was also a tough guy; he had fought in the Korean War, walked a beat as a cop, and survived everything up until this diagnosis. Now he felt helpless and dreaded sliding into the dark abyss of Alzheimer's disease. Luise was panicked with the fear of losing her husband, losing her home, and losing her hard-earned financial security. Would she even be able to live in the same neighborhood? Both husband and wife had been smashed by the wrecking ball of dementia.

Bob and Luise are typical of millions of aging American citizens. Most of them live frugally, play by the rules, and plan on enjoying a modest and pleasant retirement. But now, after the diagnosis of a long-term disability, they are overwhelmed by the staggering emotional, physical, and financial costs. This diagnosis may end up destroying their marriage, finances, and dreams.

Suddenly, their world has been turned upside down. Luise and those in her situation have many questions:

1. What can happen to Bob?
2. How will he get the health care that he needs?
3. How will he get the quality long-term care that he needs?
4. How will they live through the years between his diagnosis and his eventual death?
5. How can they protect their home so that Luise can continue to live in her community, despite the cost of Bob's multi-year care needs?
6. What will be left for Luise to live on after Bob's Alzheimer's disease has run its course?
7. What will Luise do if Bob, her always-in-charge husband, refuses to yield control of their financial and health-care decision-making?
8. Where could she find the answers to all of these questions and receive trustworthy guidance?

Luise's call to us was the best thing that she could have done. She could not have known the legal issues surrounding Bob's diagnosis. Wisely, she reached out to a trusted and experienced attorney.

Based on our many years of experience, we recommend that you follow Luise's example. Whenever you or a loved one receives a diagnosis of a long-term disease, it is very important to add an experienced elder-law attorney to your health-care and legal team.

Use This Book to Help You

When someone receives a diagnosis of dementia, it sets off an avalanche of concerns. This book is designed to help you to understand the legal issues and will also share important insights from other professionals. You've heard the term, "It takes a village to raise a child." The same can be said about helping a person who has been diagnosed with dementia. It takes a community, a family, a team of health-care providers, and experienced legal counsel to properly support and guide the person diagnosed with dementia and his/her family.

This book has been written to help you and your loved one to:

1. Find the right type of attorney to assist you in answering questions on the following topics.
2. Avoid impoverishment of the healthy spouse due to the nursing home costs of Alzheimer's care.
3. Preserve the family home for the benefit of the healthy spouse and/or an adult child with a disability from loss due to nursing home costs and Medicaid.
4. Understand nursing home Medicaid and governmentally approved asset protection planning tools.
5. Avoid the hidden traps and obstacles that can cause denial or delay in the approval of nursing home Medicaid and/or veterans' benefits.
6. Understand the difference between Medicare (neither income nor asset limitations will restrict your access to hospital and acute-care benefits) and nursing home Medicaid and Medi-Cal (income and asset limitations do restrict your access to long-term care benefits).
7. Understand short-term in-home rehabilitation benefits and nursing home rehabilitation benefits are provided under Medicare.
8. Understand the different impoverishment requirements of nursing home Medicaid and Medi-Cal benefits for either a married couple or a single individual.
9. Avoid the big mistakes caused by DIY asset-protection strategies involving asset transfers and monetary gifts to children and grandchildren.
10. Understand how to use a little-known nursing home Medicaid and Medi-Cal asset protection tool created in 1988 by Senator Ted Kennedy.
11. Determine the truth regarding wartime veterans' benefits, popularly called "Aid & Attendance."
12. Resist being victimized by annuity sales people masquerading as veterans' benefits qualification experts.
13. Discover the only safe and legal way to employ as an in-home caregiver a family member who may also be serving as power of attorney.

14. Discover the legal safeguard that can be used to give the family home to an adult child who is willing to provide caregiving services to a parent.

15. Avoid many scams that target persons with diminished mental capacity such as dementia.

16. Take legal control when a loved one with Alzheimer's is out of control.

17. Choose the right legal proxy decision-making tool (advanced directive for health care and/or finances).

18. Avoid the big mistakes in creating Special Needs Trusts for adult disabled children and/or a surviving spouse.

19. Know whether to divorce or not divorce a person diagnosed with Alzheimer's disease.

20. Understand what the honest and reliable caregiving adult child needs to know to be protected from accusations of elder abuse.

This book has been written and organized to quickly guide you to a chapter focused on specific legal concerns and recommendations. Use the table of contents to find the hottest issue that you are dealing with right now. After reading that chapter, please, read other chapters. We, the authors, know from experience that dealing with long-term care issues is a multi-disciplinary and multi-legal concept problem. This book is filled with information that you may need to know to make the right next step and to find the right attorney to help you.

Expert View: The Red Flag of Alzheimer's: A Change of Character

In 2015, Dr. William Thies was the chief medical and scientific officer for the Alzheimer's Association. Before joining the Alzheimer's Association, Dr. Thies worked at the American Heart Association. Prior to that, he held faculty positions at Indiana University in Bloomington and the University of Pittsburgh.

Q: Dr. Thies, from your point of view, what is one of the most important things that family members and professionals need to know about Alzheimer's disease and dealing with our loved ones affected by the disease?

A: The worst part of Alzheimer's disease is the later stages of the disease, and if we found ways to keep people from getting into those late stages, we would save an immense amount of human suffering, because people's quality of life goes to zero, plus the fact that the family is devastated by it, and it can rob them of all of their resources at the same time.

This disease is costing billions of dollars, and it's one of the major cost drivers in a health-care system that is becoming a major cost driver for our whole economy—and we've got to find ways to lighten the load, or it's going to wreck the whole economy.

Q: What factors should we be looking for to be able to say, "I think Chris or Mary may be suffering from Alzheimer's disease?"

A: Changes in behavior—that is the biggest thing to look for. For example, losing interest in hobbies—the guy who always got the newspaper first thing in the morning so he could do the cross-word puzzle and now he doesn't do it anymore. Look for changes in sleeping patterns. The person who was always up early and worked all day in one way or another, and now all of the sudden they're sleeping a lot during the day. Drinking—certainly whether that's a cause or an effect, I think is open to debate—but somebody who never drank and all of a sudden is drinking a significant amount. Those sorts of changes are markers of something going on.

If they have a spouse, they're going to be driving that spouse crazy because they have become totally unpredictable and undependable. They're asking them 150 times from about 3:30 to 5:30, "What's for dinner?" That's really significant.

Think about what nine out of ten people would say about your father. For example, was he funny or was he serious? Was he very punctual? Good with money? Interested in certain things? And if any of that starts to deteriorate, you should start thinking, "Gosh, this is serious."

One of the things that is very clear is that a fairly large portion of our population is living at home in early stages of Alzheimer's disease, early stages of dementia—and unless the community gathers around and tries to help them, they are in great danger. A lot of people live alone—more people are living as singles. They are those who have always been single or those who have lost a spouse, and their children have grown up and moved away, and now they are by themselves. Nobody sees their decline in cognitive function. They fall off the radar at their doctor's office, and even if they have an attorney, they fall off the radar there as well. No one calls and says, "How are you doing?" I think that's a significant worry for a substantial portion of our population. It's a societal problem.

There was the notorious case of a car dealer who sold a gentleman eight new cars in nine months because the man couldn't remember that he had recently bought a car. He would purchase the car, park it someplace, and not remember where he parked it. He had a distant memory that he needed a car and where to buy a car, but not where he parked the new car. When this problem was discovered, the car dealer was unapologetic. He said, "I sell cars, what do I know? The guy kept coming back and saying he wanted a new car, and I'm just trying to meet my customers' needs."

A man puts on a new roof after only three years—not that he has forgotten what a new roof is for, but rather he doesn't remember that he already did it.

Q: Is there anything else you would like to add?

A: Another thing that happens in families that causes havoc is that people don't see these changes as a manifestation of disease. They see it as the emergence of some sort of character flaw in their loved one. Dementia tends to aggravate a lot of the dysfunction within a family. There's real science behind the idea that people cope better with Alzheimer's if they understand that it is a disease and if they understand the sequence and they can anticipate what's coming next, and if they understand that other people have gone through this and survived. It's great to get education to people, and that's one of the reasons for the support program of the Alzheimer's Association.

CHAPTER 2

WHAT IS ALZHEIMER'S DISEASE? RECOGNIZING THE TRAJECTORY

Alzheimer's disease is a form of **dementia** characterized by the loss of memory and other intellectual abilities to the point that the disease interferes with daily life. It is the most common form of dementia, accounting for 50 to 80 percent of all dementia cases.

Dementia is a term used to describe a multitude of diseases or conditions that develop as a result of damage to the brain's nerve cells (neurons). The damage to or destruction of the neurons creates changes in an individual's memory and behavior and affects the person's ability to think clearly.

As Alzheimer's runs its course, it ultimately impairs basic bodily functions, like walking and swallowing, and finally results in death.

You can have dementia but not have Alzheimer's disease. However, you cannot have Alzheimer's and not have dementia. The term "Alzheimer's disease" comes from German physician, Dr. Alois Alzheimer. In 1906, Dr. Alzheimer presented a case history of a 51-year-old woman who was suffering from a rare brain disorder at a medical meeting. An autopsy of the woman's brain revealed the plaques and tangles that characterize Alzheimer's disease.

The Alzheimer's Journey

There are many questions that must be addressed when a loved one has Alzheimer's disease. These questions should include the following:

- How do we get health care for the patient?
- What options are available for health care?
- How are these options going to affect the patient and the family/ spouse?
- What is the long-term outlook for everyone?
- How can we protect the family assets?

Before these questions can be answered, you have to be able to identify the signs signifying the onset of Alzheimer's or dementia. Unfortunately, the initial signs of Alzheimer's or dementia are usually the most difficult to spot. It may be months or longer before family members realize that a loved one is forgetting a few too many things or is confused too frequently. Often, these first signs are dismissed as "natural aging." However, neither Alzheimer's nor dementia is a natural part of growing old.

One of the first signs of dementia is also one of the most dangerous—a growing inability to understand and control financial matters. In the oldest American generation, those who saw World War II and the Korean War, most couples' finances have been controlled by the husband; it is not unusual for the wife to have no idea of the family's financial situation. That can be particularly problematic since men, on average, decline and die earlier than their wives.

It is very important that the healthy spouse and their children be alert for signs of memory loss, which can lead to both financial vulnerability and folly. The sooner these signs are identified and reported to the family doctor and lawyer to be dealt with, the better off everyone will be. Once you suspect a loved one has some form of dementia, you should take extra care to protect their financial assets.

Memory Loss Ignored

It is difficult to determine whether memory loss is the first step of Alzheimer's or just the normal aging brain. As people age, they forget things. However, forgetting what you had for lunch last Saturday is different from forgetting that you do not have unlimited financial assets.

There is no single factor that can provide a clear sign that an adult is functioning with diminished capacity, but there are clues that, when taken together, may indicate that professional medical tests should be conducted. Knowing the factors to look for will help you to identify the signs of diminished capacity. Some of the factors include:

- change in the person's typical manner of behavior (these changes may take place over a long period of time and may not be instantly recognizable);
- unusually poor grooming or hygiene;
- short-term memory loss;
- comprehension problems;
- lack of mental flexibility;
- calculation problems;
- emotional signs of incapacity, such as emotional distress or emotional inappropriateness; and
- behavior incapacity, such as delusions or disorientation.

Do not assume that the normal aging process is the same as diminished capacity.

Once you suspect that your loved one has diminished capacity it is crucial to keep an atmosphere of open communication among family members. This will go a long way toward preventing suspicion, family fights, and potential legal claims by disgruntled family members later on.

One of your first steps is to determine who might be the best person to take control of the loved one's finances. A lawyer can assist you with the creation of the appropriate legal documents and **power of attorney for financial decision-making**. These documents give a nominated **agent** the power to make financial decisions for the affected loved one. The time to work on these plans is while the person with Alzheimer's still has sufficient capacity to make a **will**, **trust**, **power of attorney for health care**, **power of attorney for property**, and any other estate protection plans. Lawyers trained in this area of planning will work to ensure that the healthy spouse is not excessively impoverished by long-term care expenses.

Memory Loss Masked/Denied

One good way to help determine if a person is masking their memory loss is to observe the **"15-minute reset."** Look at your watch to note the time you begin a conversation with a person you suspect may be affected by

Alzheimer's or a related disorder. Often, people with excellent social skills (still common in women in their 80s and 90s) are able to hold a conversation that includes all the correct words and head nods. They are so adept at making conversation that it seems certain that there is nothing wrong with them. However, somewhere around 13 or 14 minutes they will start the conversation over again, almost as if they were playing a tape. Once again, they are so masterful with the skill that it makes you question your own memory of the conversation—as if you might have misremembered—or at the very least it makes you look around to see if someone else has entered the room to create the "reset."

You may need to get an elder-law attorney to step in and help provide guidance when there is memory loss and assistance is required but is being refused. Alzheimer's is a progressive disease and the memory loss will eventually rise to the level that the afflicted individual is no longer safe living alone.

Unsafe Alone

An estimated 800,000 individuals with Alzheimer's (or one in seven) live alone. People with Alzheimer's who live alone are exposed to higher risks—including inadequate self-care, malnutrition, untreated medical conditions, falls, wandering from home unattended, and accidental deaths—compared with those who do not live alone.

One of the signs of **younger-onset Alzheimer's** is the tendency to wander off or to become lost. This is especially dangerous because people with Alzheimer's do not act or react in the manner that a typical lost person would. Wanderers with dementia typically do not cry out for help or respond to your calls, nor will they leave many physical clues to lead you to them. Most likely, a wanderer will go to an old place of residence or a favorite location from the past.

Another danger is falling. Many elderly adults suffer falls as they age, but falls are more likely and can be more dangerous when someone has Alzheimer's disease. People with Alzheimer's or other dementias commonly suffer from impaired judgment and disorientation, and a decrease in visual and spatial perception, so their risk of falls is significantly increased.

Real-Life Story: Peter and Helen

Peter and his wife, Helen, came to see their lawyer to discuss how to deal with Helen's failing physical and mental health. They were very fortunate to have a loving and healthy adult caregiver daughter. This daughter was sacrificially serving in a way that allowed Peter and Helen to continue living in their home. She was reaching the end of her ability to care for Helen, so they needed a lawyer's advice. Peter was a successful businessman in the community and had a reputation for frugality and integrity. He was in the role of the caregiver spouse and the focus of concern was about Helen and her need for long-term care.

Over the next two years, their lawyer received a number of calls from the daughter, who had become frustrated and distressed with her father's financial decision-making. He was the healthier of the two parents and both the daughter and the family lawyer had thought that Peter's mental capacity was intact. One day, she called after she learned that her father had used a private ambulance service to take Helen to her hairdresser. Peter was deeply devoted to Helen, but he could not afford to spend $800 to have Helen transported to and from her hairdresser.

Peter and his daughter returned to see their lawyer the next week. At that appointment, the lawyer met with Peter alone and reviewed his finances with him. Peter seemed capable and intelligent at the meeting. He was able to add and subtract and respond appropriately to the questions. Nonetheless, one week later, Peter called another ambulance to take Helen to her hair appointment. The lawyer was dumbfounded—he did not realize at the time that Peter was suffering from his own rising level of dementia. He had lost his ability to understand the consequences of his decisions and acts.

A person with dementia may be able to answer questions correctly but completely fail to appreciate the consequences of the answers that he or she has given. In other words, Peter was able to say what his income was and what his assets were, but he no longer understood the difference in the effect upon him of spending $8 or $800.

People caring for a loved one with Alzheimer's should also be warned about hallucinations or delusions. It is hard to tell if these are brought on by the disease or if they are a side effect from a medication, but people with Alzheimer's have been known to suffer from one or the other or both. Of course, some will never suffer from either. If you suspect that the hallucinations or delusions are being caused by a drug your loved one is taking to treat a condition, you should contact their doctor. If the hallucinations do not upset or frighten your loved one, it may be best for the caregiver to just go along with the hallucination. In fact, validating the hallucinations is important and even healthy. However, if the hallucinations upset your loved one, consult their doctor.

Help Is Needed, but the Patient Fights Back

When someone with Alzheimer's needs help but is fighting back, it can be very hard on that person's family. Caring for a loved one with Alzheimer's can be draining, and at a certain point additional help is needed.

One option is to take advantage of a **respite care program**. These programs offer substitute caregivers and are designed to provide temporary relief for the primary caregiver from day-to- day responsibilities. Some respite programs are offered by paid health aides, while others involve volunteers from churches or other groups.

If more-intensive help is required, you can consider home-based care. This involves having a health aide provide custodial care in the home of the patient. This can be a good option when the primary caregiver is also elderly. This type of care allows patients to keep their independence for as long as possible and continue to live in their home.

Unfortunately, Medicare does not cover home health aides who provide **custodial care**, which is the type of care that an individual with Alzheimer's needs. Custodial care involves bathing, dressing, help with the housekeeping and grocery shopping, and occasionally staying overnight when needed.

Medicaid may cover portions of custodial services through a waiver program. Because the services available through the waiver program vary greatly state by state, you should contact your state office on aging to schedule a medical assessment to determine the level of service necessary to keep your loved one at home.

Another option to be aware of is adult day care. This option is great for situations in which the primary caregiver (perhaps an adult child) still works, but wants to keep the person suffering from Alzheimer's living at home. Adult day care programs provide socialization and therapeutic activities that may slow the mental decline brought on by Alzheimer's. Often these programs offer different level of care ranging from one half-day per week to full-time care, Monday through Friday. Adult day care is considered to be a stage between independent living and living in a nursing home. The person with Alzheimer's disease and their family decision makers should visit a few facilities prior to picking one to ensure the program offered is what their loved one requires at their stage of the Alzheimer's journey.

Assisted Living

There comes a point in time when your loved one will need to be placed in an assisted living facility. People in the beginning stages of Alzheimer's disease often wander off and can become lost. When that happens, it is time that the family considers assisted living options.

You need to be aware that older people with dementia who live alone are more likely to need emergency medical services because of self-neglect. Overall, people with dementia who live alone are at a greater risk of accidental death than those living with others, and this increased risk may be due to lack of recognition of harm and delays in seeking medical help.

Assisted living facilities can be the right choice for people suffering from Alzheimer's when skilled nursing is not yet needed. This is a step before a nursing home. Moving a loved one into one of these facilities often allows the healthy spouse to better cope with the difficulties of caretaking for the spouse with the disease.

The best choice may be a facility with a special care unit devoted to residents suffering from dementia. In these facilities, the staff is more experienced in handling people with dementia and more extensive care can be provided. Integrated units that have residents with dementia mixed in with otherwise healthy residents can cause problems for the residents with dementia because they may be excluded from group activities due to disruptions just when they need socialization and mental stimulation the most.

The Nursing Home

Having to place your loved one in a nursing home can be one of the hardest decisions you will ever make. But if Alzheimer's disease has progressed to the point where your loved one can no longer live alone or the primary caregiver cannot provide the level or expertise of care that is necessary, a move to a nursing home becomes necessary.

Visit several different nursing homes before narrowing down your choices. Once you have found a few facilities that stand out, visit each one several times, preferably at different times in the day and at least once during a meal. It is important to find a nursing home with an Alzheimer's special care unit.

Just like when you are looking at an assisted living facility, staff training is an important area to examine. Staff in special care units should take specialized training courses in order to be able to encourage the residents' independence and help them realize the maximum potential of their mental and physical abilities as their dementia progresses. Be aware that the special units often come at an added price.

It is important to be aware that this type of care is expensive. Fees average around $55,000 a year, nationwide, and can be as expensive as $100,000 or more. Most insurance plans do not cover this type of long-term care and neither does Medicare. Fortunately, Medicaid is available for qualified individuals. See Chapter 6.

Hospice/Death

Hospice care is a team approach to caring for an individual in the final stages of a terminal illness, such as Alzheimer's. The goal of hospice care is to provide comfort, reassurance, and support for dying patients and their family and friends.

Qualifications for hospice care require a physician's prognosis that the patient only has a life expectancy of six months. The point of hospice care is not to attempt to cure the illness but to comfort the patient, lessen the pain, and help all involved deal with the inevitable death.

Hospice care focuses on "dying well." Medicare usually covers charges for hospice services for qualified patients, and most hospice program requirements conform to Medicare and National Hospice Association Guidelines.

It is a good idea to explore the possibility of hospice care before it is needed so that you do not have to deal with this at the most emotional point of the journey. You should discuss hospice criteria with your loved one's doctor to see how willing the doctor is to certify a patient for a hospice program. If the doctor seems unwilling, consider finding another doctor. Alzheimer's is terminal, and all sufferers reach the point where the only thing left to do is to comfort and prepare them as best as possible for death.

Jo Huey, the owner of the Alzheimer's Caregiver Institute, warns us that the symptoms that signify that a patient is in the final stages of Alzheimer's disease can be as varied as the individual and his or her personality and may be affected by other unrelated health conditions. With that fact in mind, Huey notes that there have to be some guidelines to follow.

According to Huey, only about 6 percent of people with Alzheimer's (and related disorders) actually make it to the end stage of the disease. The most easily identifiable sign that someone is dying from Alzheimer's and related disorders is when he or she can no longer swallow safely (without aspiration) and has chosen not to use a feeding tube (often a legal issue, discussed further in Chapter 4). If the person is not allowed to take nutrition or hydration orally safely, he or she is unlikely to survive for a long period of time. You should be aware that it is advisable, at the very least, to have a speech therapist make this determination.

Huey says the second most common qualifier for hospice is when there is a significant weight loss even though the person is eating meals regularly. She notes that the majority of people with Alzheimer's and related disorders actually die from infection. Common examples are:

1. sepsis from undiagnosed urinary tract or other infection (abscessed tooth, etc.) that enters the blood and can't be stopped if it has progressed too far; and

2. pneumonia, sometimes from aspiration or an illness or virus, that, because the person cannot communicate his or her illness, it goes undetected until it has progressed too far.

True-Life Story: Jo Huey, owner of the Alzheimer's Caregiver Institute

Jo Huey's mother was 84 years old and had vascular dementia. She hated going to the hospital ER, which was the legal procedure required if she became ill in the assisted living community where she lived. When she went to the ER, Jo would hurry there from out of state, and, in the meantime, one of the relatives (sometimes Jo's sister who also had medical POA) would accompany her. They would have the doctor, attending ER physician, or medical residency student call and talk to Jo because the family did not want her mother to have an MRI, CAT scan, or any extensive diagnostic procedures that terrified her.

In August 2006, an angry physician told Jo that he was trained to "treat" people in the ER, and if Jo wanted to decline treatment for her mother, then she should put her mother in hospice and stop bringing her to the ER. Jo called hospice and learned that her mother qualified for the service. Her doctor was willing to sign for it and she was recertified again in six months. She happened to be doing quite well in August of 2007 when the recertification came up again. Although she still qualified, a physician's signature was required for recertification. The physician declined to recertify her because, "she could live another 10 years."

Jo called her physician, who just happened to be someone with whom Jo had grown up, and asked him why he wouldn't recertify, and he gave her the same answer. Jo asked what to do about ER and extensive diagnostic procedures and he said something to the effect of, "You can just come here and stop those things or tell the community not to send her to the ER (he was unfamiliar with the community's regulations or didn't care). When Jo told him her mother qualified for hospice and that Jo wanted her recertified, he angrily accused Jo of "using the system" (Jo's mother was in a private pay community and had insurance that supplemented her Medicare). Jo retorted that even if they were using the system, it was none of his business that Jo wanted her mother to have hospice. He asked Jo how she was going to do that without his signature and Jo told him that she would call another physician in the same town "whom we both knew" and change doctors. He said, "You wouldn't really do that." Jo said, "Without a signature you will be getting a fax to transfer records in the next 15 minutes." He was furious and signed the hospice certification.

Just 19 days later, Jo's mother died in her sleep following a massive stroke and four days of being comatose. She died in her own bed in the assisted living community where she had been dancing and smiling less than a week prior.

Huey stresses the importance of making certain that lawyers individualize health care power of attorney documents to meet the specific needs and desires of the person with Alzheimer's disease and the loved ones who are responsible for the decisions when the person can no longer make them alone.

It is a good idea to register your loved one in the MedicAlert Safe Return program run by the Alzheimer's Association. Members of the MedicAlert Safe Return program are issued an ID bracelet or other form of jewelry with the association's logo on one side and the individual's identification number on the other side to aid in identification.

Adult children living with a parent suffering from dementia can put a baby monitor in the parent's bedroom so that they can hear them get up in the middle of the night. It is also a good idea to put safety devices in your home and to warn the neighbors of the possibility of wandering and ask them to keep an eye out.

Memory Loss Ignored: Checklist of Signs/Issues

There is no single factor that can provide a clear sign that an adult is functioning with diminished capacity, but there are clues that, when taken together, may indicate that professional medical tests should be conducted. Knowing the factors to look for will help you to identify the signs of diminished capacity. Some of the factors include:

❑ change in the person's typical manner of behavior (these changes may take place over a long period of time and may not be instantly recognizable);

❑ unusually poor grooming or hygiene;

❑ short-term memory loss;

❑ comprehension problems;

❑ lack of mental flexibility;

❑ calculation problems;

❑ emotional signs of incapacity, such as emotional distress or emotional inappropriateness; and

❑ behavior incapacity, such as delusions or disorientation.

17

Moving to an Assisted Living Facility: Checklist

Family members moving a loved one to an assisted living facility should ask the following questions about the facility to ensure they are making an informed choice.

❑ Is the facility or program licensed? Check with your state's guidelines to see what kind of licensing is required.

❑ What is the environment like? What are the common areas like? Is there an enclosed yard or patio that is a safe area that an Alzheimer's patient could not wander away from? Is the atmosphere friendly? You want your loved one to be as comfortable as possible.

❑ What kinds of activities are offered? Ask to see the activities calendar. Is there a full-time activities director? It is important to find a place that offers a wide variety of activities to provide social interaction and mental stimulation.

❑ What is the staff-to-patient ratio? Generally, look for one certified nurse's aide (CNA) per five residents during the day, and a ratio of one to 10 at night.

❑ How well trained are the staff? Look for a facility where staff instruction includes interaction with an instructor, group discussions, and role-playing activities to ensure a quality staff that is ready to help your loved one.

❑ Does the facility have a special Alzheimer's unit? Some facilities have residents with a variety of needs, while others have a unit for people with dementia, and others are completely dedicated to residents with dementia.

❑ What medical care is available?

❑ Is a contract necessary? Alzheimer's progresses at unpredictable rates, so avoid contracts longer than 30 days in case you need to switch to a nursing home sooner.

When a Nursing Home Is Required: Checklist

You should look for the following qualities from a nursing home with a special unit before agreeing to pay the higher rate:

- ❑ Does the facility confirm the Alzheimer's diagnoses of all incoming residents?

- ❑ Is the staff aware of the progressive nature of Alzheimer's disease, and how do they address the expected changes in the mental and physical abilities of the residents?

  - Are all of the employees in the special unit (the housekeepers, maintenance workers, etc.) given some training regarding Alzheimer's?

  - Are the buildings and grounds designed for people suffering from Alzheimer's disease?

  - Are the resident activities appropriate for people with Alzheimer's?

Expert View: Don't Be Confounded by a Loved One's Confabulations

Dr. Nishad "Nick" Nadkarni is a licensed physician and surgeon in Wisconsin and Illinois. In addition, he is certified as a general and forensic psychiatrist. His professional experience includes working in private practice and, starting in 2004, working full time for the Circuit Court of Cook County, Forensic Clinical Services. The Forensic Clinical Services are primarily charged with determining clinical competencies, like fitness to stand trial and fitness for medications, for people indicted or charged with criminal offenses. Part of the training is being able to understand the different levels of capacity from the standpoint of legal definitions of capacity; for example, testamentary capacity, contractual capacity, donative capacity, and other criminal and civil competencies.

Q: Would you say based on your experience that it's common for someone to admit to their dementia or their memory issues?

A: I would say it is *not* common, and almost always it is outright denied, even in the face of tremendous contradictory evidence.

Q: Despite short-term memory issues, can people develop a masking technique?

A: Yes. One of the techniques is confabulation—the insertion of details to fill in holes in the memory. For example, if I really couldn't remember what happened this morning, I might give you what sounds like a reasonable explanation. You could ask me, "Dr. Nick, what did you do this morning?" and I could say, very convincingly, "I ate breakfast—I had two eggs, bacon, and toast," and even with that I may be confabulating. I really can't remember what I did—but I'm going to fill in the detail and not even be aware that I'm telling you something that is confabulated or made up. It's very possible that someone can give you a complete rundown of what they did even though they have absolutely no actual remembrance. People will tell you what meets social expectations and what you would expect to hear.

Whatever that person may be talking to you about, it may have absolutely no basis in truth. Without reliable collateral information, you would not know that. Thus, when you hear about a person's activities of daily living and independence, it's important to receive collateral information to back up what someone who is confabulating is telling you. The only way that you would know that there were problems is by doing some formal testing.

Q: Over the years as a forensic psychiatrist, have you had the opportunity to observe a large number of families of persons with dementia?

A: Yes, several thousand.

Q: What do you wish more people knew about dementia?

A: There is an old saying in medicine: get consultation, get consultation, and then get consultation. Whenever there is a question about mental capacity, to protect everyone's interests—primarily the person affected by dementia—I wish more people would seek professional consultation.

The other thing that concerns me is most people's basic understanding of dementia. It can be very difficult to assess. For example, early-onset Parkinson's disease has a dementia component. These types of dementias will present themselves very atypically and might affect a 58-year-old man who is having a bizarre complex of symptoms that may not be understood unless professionally evaluated. They are not necessarily affecting the short-term memory of the individual.

Also, there are certain things that cause *reversible* memory impairment, like major depressive disorder—what's called the pseudodementia of depression. If the depression is bad enough, the thinking can be so slow that they're unable to take in and retain information, and in a sense it dissipates. But antidepressants can reverse that. This is a very common phenomenon in the elderly. In addition, many older people are affected by hypothyroidism, which can increase the appearance of dementia.

People need to be aware that dementia is more than just memory impairment. Look for clusters of problems with cognitive processing, memory processing, behavioral processing and control, emotional problems, emotional control, impulsivity, activities of daily living, sequencing and arranging, what we call executive functioning, ability to communicate, ability to feel secure with familiar people. All of these things may deteriorate in dementia and some may be subtle. If you have a bona fide doubt about a person's capacity, then if possible, ask an appropriate healthcare professional for an evaluation.

On the other hand, just because a person is on a certain medication doesn't mean that they have incapacity. A person may be taking Aricept®, Namenda® or some other medicine often prescribed for dementia—but they may still have testamentary or contractual or donative capacity. A medicine doesn't equate a diagnosis, and a diagnosis does not equate a capacity issue.

Q: Describe a typical evaluation.

A: When I do an examination, I break it up into three phases. First, I like to see the person in their own home. I am able to look at safety issues. I then spend 30–45 minutes asking people what they think is important. I then go through a formal evaluation of psychiatric history, any history of psychiatric symptoms, memory problems, history of substance abuse, current medications, allergies, medical problems, and that they understand why they're taking their medications. We'll often go through a brief legal history as well.

21

Secondly, I would make an examination called a Mini-Mental State Examination, or MMSE, which is a screening tool for the grossest levels of dementia. At that point I have a quantitative number that may or may not mean something, but courts seem to appreciate an ability to quantify. I personally think that the mental status observations on the person's thought flow is more significant, but I do a Mini-Mental State Exam.

The third phase involves understanding of one's finances. I go through a series of questions to ascertain someone's general knowledge about how much they make in a year, how much their home costs, how much their car costs, etc. Then I address areas of insight, judgment, and impulse control regarding safety issues. What should you do if the house smells like gas? When is it appropriate to call emergency services? When should you go to an emergency room?

I'm interested in looking at whether they're jumping from one-time frame to another without any logical connection. That tells me whether the person is confused regarding significant key events in their life and whether or not they're able to identify or tag certain areas and build a story around those areas.

So I do much more than just asking somebody to add two plus two. It is a comprehensive evaluation that allows me to see *how* people are thinking, in addition to *what* they're thinking.

CHAPTER 3

ALZHEIMER'S DISEASE AND HOW TO FIND A SAVVY ATTORNEY

When it comes to finding an attorney who understands the specific issues of Alzheimer's and the law, it is important to understand that in today's world, most lawyers are focused in specific areas of the law.

You most likely have experience with doctors. These days, when you have a sudden medical concern, you typically enter the world of health care through a gatekeeper—either a primary care physician, an urgent care center, or a hospital emergency room. After you have been given a preliminary examination, the gatekeeper will either treat you or tell you that you need to be referred to a specialist. Most specialists are concentrated in urban areas.

Just like the world of health care, modern legal practice follows this pattern. You are looking for an attorney who has focused his or her study and practice within a very complex niche. Most such attorneys are located within urban areas. What you need to find is an attorney who has substantial experience in the issues of aging, dementia, long-term health care, Medicare, Medicaid, and nursing-home asset protection.

There is a distinct difference between an estate planner who is focused in wills and trusts and an elder law estate planner who is focused not only in wills and trusts, but also in the issues of health care during the aging trajectory. We call that trajectory *the elder care journey*. You are looking for an attorney who is focused on giving advice not only about estate planning, but also about how to survive and thrive during the aging process.

Such an attorney needs to understand a wide variety of issues that face clients as they become senior citizens. They need to understand how health care will be provided for their clients and how health care for seniors is paid for in the United States. The attorney with the appropriate experience will be able to show clients that if done correctly, their elder-law-informed estate plan can have profoundly positive benefits for the client and family—even while the client is still alive. The client estate plan should not be solely focused on the death of the client but rather on the entire aging trajectory. That means that the plan should be designed to protect the healthy surviving spouse after the death of the husband or wife. The attorney you seek should understand that how an estate plan is created, funded, and financed can make an enormous difference in the quality of the client's life and the lives of those left behind. You are looking for an attorney who has substantial experience in helping people make life, death, and health-care decisions.

A recommended first step in finding a qualified elder law attorney would be to go to the website www.naela.org. That is the website of the National Academy of Elder Law Attorneys—an organization of attorneys who are focused in the issue of elder law. The organization refers to itself by the nickname of NAELA (pronounced "nayla"). According to the organization website:

> Members of the National Academy of Elder Law Attorneys are experienced and trained in working with the legal problems of aging Americans and individuals of all ages with disabilities. Elder law planning includes helping such persons and their families with planning for incapacity and long-term care, Medicaid and Medicare coverage (including coverage of nursing home and home care), health and long-term care insurance, and health-care decision-making. It also includes drafting of special needs and other trusts, the selection of long-term care providers, home care and nursing home problem solving, retiree health and income benefits, retirement housing, and fiduciary services or representation.

NAELA is a nonprofit association established in 1987 that assists lawyers, bar organizations, and others. It has members throughout the United States and in Canada, Australia, and the United Kingdom.

The NAELA website states under the consumer resources tab,

> Elder law attorneys use a variety of legal tools and techniques to meet the goals and objectives of their clients. Using a holistic

24

approach, elder law attorneys often work with other professionals in various fields to provide quality service and assure that clients' needs are met. In conjunction with other professionals, an elder law attorney can address several issues such as:

1. general estate planning

2. planning for incapacity with alternative decision-making documents and planning for possible long-term care needs, including nursing home care

3. locating the right care facility and coordinating financial resources to pay for the cost of care

4. ensuring the clients' right to quality care—all part of the elder law practice

NAELA members are committed to continuing their legal education and enhancing the quality of services they provide their clients.

It is important to note that just because an attorney has joined NAELA does not necessarily mean that the attorney has sufficient experience and qualifications. An attorney can join NAELA simply by contacting the organization and paying the membership fee. The attorney is then authorized to claim membership in the premier elder law organization in the United States. You must dig deeper to determine the qualifications of the specific attorney before making a decision to engage that attorney to represent you or your family member with Alzheimer's disease.

The NAELA organization understands the need for consumers to be properly represented. The NAELA website includes a section entitled "Questions & Answers" when looking for an elder law attorney. The organization recommends that you ask lots of questions before selecting an attorney who represents him/herself as capable in elder law.

The NAELA website states,

Legal issues that affect people as they age are growing in number. Our laws and regulations are becoming more complex, and each state has different laws. Actions taken with regard to a single matter may have unintended legal effects.

It is important for attorneys working with seniors and their families, to have a broad understanding of the laws that may have an impact on a given situation in order to avoid future problems. Elder law encompasses many different fields of law. Some of these include:

1. preservation/transfer of assets to avoid spousal impoverishment when one spouse enters a nursing home
2. Medicare claims and appeals
3. Social Security and disability claims and appeals
4. supplemental and long-term health insurance issues
5. tax planning
6. disability planning, including use of durable powers of attorney, living trusts, living wills for financial management and health-care decisions, and other means of delegating management and decision-making to another in case of incapacity or incompetency
7. access to health care in a managed care environment
8. conservatorships and guardianships
9. estate planning, including planning for the management of one's estate during life and its disposition on death, through the use of trusts, wills, and other planning documents
10. probate administration of estates
11. administration and management of trusts
12. long-term care placements in nursing homes and other long-term care communities
13. nursing home issues, including questions of patients' rights and nursing home quality
14. elder abuse and fraud recovery cases
15. retirement, including public and private retirement benefits, survivor benefits, and pension benefits
16. health law
17. mental health law

Most attorneys do not specialize in every one of these areas; therefore, when an attorney says he or she practices elder law, find out which of these matters the attorney handles. You will want to hire the attorney who *regularly* handles matters in the area of law of concern to your particular case and who will know enough about the other fields to question whether the action being taken might be affected by laws in any of the other areas of law. For example, if you're going to rewrite your will and your spouse is ill, the attorney needs to know enough about Medicaid/Medi-Cal to know whether there are legal issues with regard to your spouse's inheritance.

Attorneys who primarily work with seniors appreciate the complex financial and social decisions their clients face. Elder law attorneys bring to the practice a knowledge of their clients that allows them and their staff to ignore the myths relating to aging and the competence of seniors. At the same time, they will take into account and empathize with some of the true physical and mental difficulties that often accompany the aging process. They are usually tied into a formal or informal system of social workers, geriatric care managers, psychologists, and other professionals who may be of assistance to you or your loved one.

Finding an Elder Law Attorney

There are many places to find an attorney in your city or state who specializes in working with the problems facing people as they age. Check with local agencies to obtain good quality local referrals. Some of the groups you may want to contact include:

1. Alzheimer's Association
2. American Association of Retired Persons (AARP)
3. your area Agency/Council on Aging
4. hospital or nursing home social services
5. state or local bar associations
6. support groups for specific diseases such as Alzheimer's or Parkinson's

If you know any attorneys, ask them for a referral to an elder law attorney. An attorney is in a good position to know who handles such issues and whether that person is regarded as a good attorney. Such people are often the best and safest source of referrals.

Ask Questions First

Take the time to interview prospective attorneys. Not every attorney is right for every client. The attorney/client relationship must be built on mutual trust and understanding.

Ask lots of questions before selecting an elder law attorney, including questions about fees and services. You don't want to end up in the office of an attorney who can't help you!

Start with the initial phone call. It is not unusual to speak to a secretary, receptionist, or office manager during an initial call, before actually meeting with the attorney. If so, ask this person these questions.

1. How long has the attorney been in practice?
2. Does his/her practice emphasize a particular area of law?
3. How long has he/she been in this area of law?
4. What percentage of his/her practice is devoted to elder law?
5. Is there a fee for the first consultation, and if so, how much is it?
6. Given the nature of the problem, what information should we bring with us to the initial consultation?

The answers to your questions will assist you in determining whether that particular attorney has the qualifications that are important to you for a successful attorney/client relationship. If you have a specific legal issue that requires immediate attention, be sure to inform the office of this during the initial telephone conversation.

Once You Have Found an Elder Law Attorney

When you have found an appropriate attorney, make an appointment. During the initial phone consultation, you will be asked to give an overview of the reason you are seeking assistance, so be sure to organize and bring any information they request regarding your situation. See the checklist at the end of this chapter for some questions to ask at your first appointment.

Discussing Fees

There are many different ways of charging fees, and each attorney will choose to work differently. Be aware of how your attorney charges. You will also want to know how often you will be billed. Some attorneys bill weekly, some bill monthly, some bill upon completion of the work, and some bill in advance. Ask about these matters at the initial conference, so there will be no surprises. If you don't understand, ask again. If you need clarification, say so. It is very important that you feel comfortable in this area.

Some attorneys charge by the hour, with different hourly rates for work performed by attorneys, paralegals, and secretaries. If this is the case, know what the different rates are. Other attorneys charge a flat fee for all or some of the services—this is not unusual. Your attorney might use a combination of these billing methods.

In addition to fees, many attorneys will charge you out-of-pocket expenses. These expenses typically include charges for copies, postage, messenger fees, court fees, deposition fees, long distance telephone calls, and other such costs. Find out if there will be any other incidental costs.

The attorney may ask for a "retainer." This is money paid before the attorney starts working on your case. It is usually placed in a trust account and each time the attorney bills you, he or she is paid from that account. Expenses may be paid directly from the trust account as well. The size of the retainer may range from a small percentage of the estimated cost to the full amount. In many cases, the total fee will end up higher than the retainer.

Get It in Writing

Once you decide to hire the attorney, ask that your arrangement be put in writing. This is called an "engagement agreement." The document can be a letter or a formal contract. It should spell out what services the attorney will perform for you and what the fee and expense arrangements will be.

Remember—even if your agreement is only oral and is not put in writing, you still have made a legal contract, and you are responsible for all charges for work done by the attorney and his or her staff.

Make It a Good Experience

Again, from the NAELA website:

A positive and open relationship between attorney and client benefits everyone. The key is communication. The communication starts with asking the kinds of questions suggested in this article. Use the answers to the questions as a guide not only as to the attorney's qualifications, but also as a way of determining whether you can comfortably work with this person. If your concerns are given short shrift, if you don't like the answers to the questions, if you don't like the attorney's reaction to being asked those questions, or if you simply do not feel relaxed with this particular person, do not hire that person. Only if you're satisfied with the attorney you have hired from the very start, will you trust him/her to the best job for you. Only if you have established a relationship of open communication, will you be able to resolve any difficulties that may arise between the two of you. If you take the time to make sure that you're happy right at the beginning, you can make this a productive experience for both you and the attorney. You will thank yourself, and your attorney will thank you.

The authors wish to express their thanks to NAELA for their support and guidance to both consumers and the attorneys who seek to serve them. We highly recommend that you follow the guidance provided above as you seek the right legal counsel.

The NAELA website at www.naela.org has a Find-a-Lawyer search function. After you go to the website, you can fill in basic information such as the ZIP code of the individual who would become the client. The search function will provide you with a list of attorneys most geographically appropriate for the prospective client.

Caution: Just because the search function provides you with the name and contact information of an attorney does not mean that the attorney is the most experienced or capable attorney for your situation. Please follow the recommendations within this chapter and the following checklist so as to be able to independently determine whether any specific attorney meets your needs.

Checklist of Attorney Interview Questions

❑ How many attorneys are in this office/firm?

_____

❑ Who will actually handle the case?

_____

❑ How many cases similar to my case have you/your firm handled during the last month? Or year? Or career?

_____

❑ Is the attorney a member of the local bar association or other professional associations?

_____

❑ How are fees computed and charged?

_____

❑ What will it take to resolve this problem?

_____

❑ What is the probability of success?

_____

❑ What are our alternative courses of action?

_____

_____

❑ What are the advantages and disadvantages of each alternative?

_____

_____

❑ What is an estimate of the cost to resolve the problem, and how long will it take?

_____

_____

_____

❑ What are the expected benefits to be received from the recommended solution?

_____

_____

_____

CHAPTER 4

MAKING SENSE OF ADVANCE HEALTH CARE AND FINANCIAL POWERS OF ATTORNEYS, LIVING WILLS, DO NOT RESUSCITATE (DNR) FORMS, AND MORE

People know that they are going to die—someday. Nonetheless, most people do not act as if they believe that they are actually going to die or get a long-term illness. The evidence for that statement is that 85 percent of the adult population does not have a simple **will** or **advance directives** in place that allow their chosen **agent** legally to make financial and health-care decisions on their behalf. Nonetheless, 100 percent of people are going to die, and the majority of individuals who live beyond the age of 75 will need long-term care at home, in an assisted living facility, or in a nursing home.

We use the term **"incapacity"** to refer to someone who is not mentally fit or able to safely handle their own decision-making. None of us wants to lose our independence or control of our finances. People do not plan for their own incapacity because they do not want to believe that they may reach the point of being unable to control of their own finances or make responsible decisions about their health care. Failure to have the courage to plan for future incapacity is one of the greatest personal mistakes of our retirees and seniors.

To-Do Checklist

❑ Know what an advance health-care directive is

❑ Know what an advance directive for financial power is

❑ Know what can happen without an advance directive

❑ Know what a living will is (compared to a will)

❑ Know what it means to be an agent within a power of attorney

❑ Understand what a Do Not Resuscitate (DNR) order really means

❑ Understand the importance of choosing honest and reliable agents

❑ Know what a Physician's Order for Life Sustaining Treatment (POLST) is

What Does "Incapacity" Really Mean?

The requirements differ from state to state, but "**capacity**" generally means the mental ability to perceive and appreciate relevant facts, to understand the consequences of those facts, and to make rational decisions. "Incapacity," then, describes the lack of those abilities.

As elder law attorneys, we have presented **health-care power of attorney** language to several thousand people. We have learned that when we use the word "incapacity," most people think it is a rare event; most often, they think it is the state of being unconscious. Therefore, when lawyers talk to clients about making a power of attorney for incapacity, the client has a hard time imagining anything but the rarest occurrences that could render them unconscious. In reality, however, people alive today face an aging trajectory in which the majority will progressively lose their ability to make good decisions. For those who reach the age of 85, at least one-third to one-half will not have sufficient mental capability to make good decisions about both their finances and their health care. *That* is incapacity.

Make sure to ask your lawyer to explain to you exactly what incapacity means—especially in the context of Alzheimer's disease. This is a very complicated and very important issue. Don't be afraid to ask for further clarification! When you choose someone as your agent under a health- care power of attorney or **financial power of attorney**, do not choose emotionally, or by birth order. For example, many parents choose their oldest child even though that may not be the best choice. Make sure to choose honest, reliable, and capable family members or professionals to make decisions on your behalf. Most people choose a family member; if you do so, be sure to consider carefully and choose one who loves you and shares your values.

Advance Directives for Financial Decisions and Health-Care Decisions

Advance directives are documents such as a **living will**, power of attorney for health care, **power of attorney for property**, and **Do Not Resuscitate order (DNR)**. People sign these forms primarily because they want to avoid unwanted resuscitation and other "heroic measures" when there is no hope of recovery and returning to an enjoyable life.

These are very important documents when dealing with any serious health-care issues, including long-term illness and Alzheimer's disease. These documents allow people to communicate health-care preferences ahead of time, so that when they lose the capacity to make or communicate their own decisions, their wishes can still be communicated. It is important to remember that an advance directive has to be signed while a person still possesses the mental capacity to sign legal documents that authorize someone else to make future decisions on their behalf.

Simply filling out an advance directive is not enough. Later in this chapter, there will be a discussion about the difference between a *powerful* power of attorney and a *less powerful* standard-form power of attorney.

What Can Happen Without an Advance Directive?

If a loved one does not have a living will and has not created a power of attorney, and dementia such as Alzheimer's disease has progressed to the point where the individual is no longer competent to make decisions (incapacity), you may be forced to hire an attorney to seek a **guardianship** over your loved one. In a guardianship proceeding, evidence must be submitted to convince a judge of the need to appoint the proper person to make decisions on behalf of your loved one. Guardianships may often be lengthy, expensive, and embarrassing and involve contentious court hearings to determine competency of the loved one and who should be appointed the guardian.

Worse yet, if your loved one is determined to be **incompetent**, another hearing will be held. The court will appoint a **conservator** to handle the individual's financial affairs, and/or a guardian will be appointed to tend to their personal and health-care needs. (Conservatorship and guardianship are discussed in more detail in Chapter 9.) While most states' laws encourage the courts to appoint family members as conservators and guardians, court involvement can be expensive and may impose cumbersome supervision on the individual and the conservator and guardian.

If state law permits, when an incapacitated patient is in the hospital and does not have a living will or a power of attorney, the attending physician may appoint a surrogate decision maker who would then be authorized to make health-care decisions for the patient. These decisions include whether to forego life-sustaining treatment.

Many clients and their family members have told the authors about doctors and/or hospital staff who ignored the refusal of life-prolonging care wishes of a now-deceased loved one. These individuals stated that they had insisted that their loved one did not want life-prolonging treatment, but nonetheless a doctor ordered feeding tubes, ventilators, and other life-prolonging measures.

Fortunately, there are ways to prevent "wrongful resuscitation" and other unwanted procedures. To avoid such medical interventions, you should have an attorney help you create the types of written advance directives that are discussed below (health-care power of attorney, living will, and/or a DNR in appropriate circumstances) and insist that the advance directives are placed in all of his or her medical records. Make sure that the physician is well aware of the existence of such documents.

You and your loved one with Alzheimer's should have "the talk" with all family members and the doctor. The substance of this talk will be your loved one's feelings regarding life-sustaining treatment in the event that there is no hope of recovery, and making sure that everyone is very aware of his or her wishes. It is important to have the "Final Arrangement Conversation" sooner rather than later. Alzheimer's is a fatal disease, and it is in everyone's best interest to find out how the person suffering from the disease feels about life-prolonging treatment.

In addition, you should choose an "**advocate**" to be his or her health-care power of attorney and/or surrogate decision maker. An advocate is someone who can look a medical professional in the eye and insist that certain wishes be carried out. It is recommended that you look through his or her family and friends and choose someone who can be trusted to do so.

It's important to know that there is substantial legal authority for health-care directives to be followed. In fact, it is now legally considered inappropriate when a hospital performs a wrongful resuscitation. The Centers for Medicare and Medicaid Services (CMS) emphasizes that patients have the right to make decisions regarding their long-term health care and that those decisions should be respected by physicians and hospitals.

People with Alzheimer's disease who are in the early or mild stage of dementia may retain their mental facilities for months or even years. At this stage they may experience only short episodes of impaired mental function and can still receive, understand, and evaluate information. More importantly, for purposes of advance directives, these individuals can still make rational decisions and evaluate legal documents.

Unfortunately, Alzheimer's progresses, and it does so at a different rate for everyone. As the disease advances, episodes of dementia may become more frequent and may last longer.

Eventually, the disease will reach the point where the individual may no longer meet a state's legal test for "capacity" and will no longer be able to execute a valid and enforceable legal document, such as an advance directive. The requirements differ from state to state, but as explained above, "capacity" generally means the mental ability to perceive and appreciate relevant facts and make rational decisions.

In the case of Alzheimer's disease, advance planning should begin at diagnosis so that the person with dementia can participate as much as possible. Advance planning also avoids the issue of family members having to make important decisions during a crisis on behalf of the individual suffering from Alzheimer's.

If you do not act quickly, your loved one runs the risk of being deemed "**incompetent**," at which point a court will have to step in and appoint a guardian.

Mental Capacity

There are two general levels of legal (mental) capacity. The mental capacity sufficient to create a will or other estate plan is called "**testamentary capacity**." Testamentary capacity is necessary for the execution of a valid will and/or testamentary trust and is defined as sound mind and memory.

To be of sound mind and memory, people must:

- know they are making a will
- know and remember their family members who would most normally inherit
- know what they own, and how much of what kind of assets they own
- make the disposition of their property according to their own plan

---

Real-Life Story: The Problem of Doing It Yourself

In this Internet age when seemingly everything is available online, many people may be tempted to download their own living will or health-care power of attorney instead of consulting a lawyer. The forms seem to be self-explanatory, but they are actually more complex than they look.

We have seen self-created advance directives which will not be acceptable to health-care providers. One client had initialed all the available choices in regard to end-of-life decisions rather than simply choosing one. That would make the document impossible to interpret in the event of an emergency health-care decision.

Another client brought in a form on which the person named as the principal had not signed the form. Rather, the daughter (the client's agent) had signed it where the principal was supposed to sign. Often, clients bring in forms that are not witnessed or are witnessed by interested parties. Most often, state laws do not allow anyone who is being named an agent or successor agent to act as witness of the document.

In short, if one can imagine an error that could be made on these forms, there is an individual who will make that error. In the arena of advance directives, the do-it-yourself approach can be a waste of time, or worse.

Another level of capacity is termed "**contractual capacity**" and is required for the execution of living trusts, deeds, and powers of attorney. Contractual capacity is defined as the ability to comprehend and understand the terms and effect of the contract.

It is a good idea to ask your lawyer to add the full contact information of agents into the power of attorney. This simple act makes it easier for health-care providers to communicate with the agent during a time of crisis.

Living Wills

Based on our years of experience, we would always recommend that our clients appoint honest, reliable, and capable family members as their agents under powers of attorney.

But in the event that there is no one chosen to serve as agent with power of attorney, then the alternative is a living will. A valid health-care power of attorney usually trumps a living will. Living wills are often prepared by chaplains and social workers within the hospital.

A living will sets out the Alzheimer's patient's choices for future medical decisions, such as the use of artificial life support, and is used to instruct medical personnel of the person's wishes. A living will takes effect only when two doctors certify in writing that the person is irreversibly ill or critically injured and near death. The living will empowers the health-care community to determine when someone with a terminal illness should not have life-prolonging treatment.

It is important to be aware of the defined terms and to make sure you understand their meanings when filling out a living will. For example, many people may not be aware that when they say they want "**sustenance**" they are *actually requiring* the use of a feeding tube and hydration.

Many states require that a power of attorney contain a written statement authorizing the agent and health-care community to withhold a feeding tube. Generally, a living will does not prohibit the use of a feeding tube. Use a power of attorney for health care if your loved one does not want a feeding tube. Not only will that help ensure their wishes are met but it will remove any guilt from the family by taking the decision-making process out of their hands.

Real-Life Story: Terri Schiavo Case

One of the leading cases dealing with advance directives is the Terri Schiavo case. In 1990, Terri Schiavo, a young woman, suffered cardiac arrest and went into a persistent vegetative state due to brain damage from prolonged oxygen loss. As she had no advance directives of any kind, Schiavo was kept alive for 15 years by artificial hydration and nutrition given through a feeding tube while her parents and her estranged husband, who disagreed about whether to keep her on life support, engaged in a long and contentious legal battle. If she had had a living will or power of attorney in place, it would have served as a written expression of her intent and could have put an end to the controversy.

Certainly, the expression of intent regarding removal of life support in writing is a circumstance that will put a family's mind at ease. However, it is preferable that a family, an Alzheimer's patient, or a client use a *durable power of attorney for health care* rather than a *living will*.

There is always the danger that a living will may end up in front of an ethics committee regarding the terminal condition of the patient. Make sure your attorney understands your loved one's intent and drafts a powerful living will that spells out that intent.

Power of Attorney

Some of the most important documents your loved one with Alzheimer's can have created are **durable powers of attorney** for financial matters and health-care decisions. These documents are very important because they allow a family member or trusted friend to have legal authority to carry out the wishes of people suffering from Alzheimer's once they are no longer able to speak or act for themselves.

Powers of attorney are relatively simple, inexpensive legal documents that basically allow another person to act for the person signing the documents. The person granting the authority by signing the documents is called the *principal* and the person being granted the authority is the *agent* or *attorney of fact*. This person stands in for the principal and is authorized to take almost any action for the principal *so long as that action is included in the powers of attorney document*.

A power of attorney has been described as a legal document that grants the authority to another person to become the principal's "legal clone." A "durable" power of attorney continues in effect after the principal becomes incapacitated and is unable to supervise and direct the agent.

The mental capacity required for appointment of a power of attorney agent is different from the capacity required to manage one's own affairs. It is possible to be capable of appointing an agent yet lack the capacity to make certain types of personal decisions. Individuals appointing an agent must be able to comprehend that they have a choice whether or not to appoint an agent, and they must be capable of making that choice. Many people who have a diagnosis of Alzheimer's disease and may be taking medications often continue to have sufficient mental capacity to know whom they love and trust to handle financial and health decisions.

Powerful Versus Powerless Powers of Attorney

While it is true that powers of attorney are great tools for anyone who needs to empower an agent to act on the principal's behalf, they are only as powerful as the powers included by the person drafting it. Too often, lawyers and non-lawyers use the standard-form power of attorney provided by their home state. In cases of people with long-term care needs, an elder law attorney will often add non-traditional powers that may turn out to be very important in authorizing long- term care asset protection strategies, or in allowing family members to be compensated for providing important caregiving services to the principal.

Even though a power may be legally available and necessary, if a power is not noted in the power of attorney document, agents are powerless to use the missing tool.

The standard health-care powers of attorney that are typically available are not very powerful in the long-term care environment. That is because they are documents cobbled together by various political factions, religious organizations, disability lobbyists, and medical groups, and then written by lawyers.

The standard powers are usually designed to authorize an agent to make health-care decisions in the event of emergency and/or a hospitalization crisis. When you are faced with decisions about providing supportive non-health-care decisions in the home of a loved one, or to qualify a loved one for veterans' benefits or nursing-home Medicaid/Medi-Cal, you need a more power-filled, or powerful, power of attorney.

"Five Wishes"

Very few health-care powers of attorney are written by health-care providers, social workers, or those who deal with more of the emotional side of human beings as they're going through their final life decision-making. There is, however, a document called Five Wishes. This is the closest thing to a health-care power of attorney for the emotional side of care.

Almost every state has a statutory power of attorney written by attorneys. Many times, it is only good within the boundaries of that state and doesn't work well in another state. Five Wishes, on the other hand, is the most widely accepted form of power of attorney in the country. There is no other health-care power of attorney promulgated by any state legislature that is as widely accepted. Ask your lawyer if Five Wishes meets the statutory requirements of your state. While it is not designed to deal with governmental benefits such as Medicaid or veterans' benefits, it is an excellent and inexpensive self-help power of attorney for health care.

Five Wishes was written with the help of the American Bar Association's Commission on Law and Aging and national leading experts in end-of-life care and with a religious background. The creator of the document was inspired by working with Mother Teresa and wanted to create a way for patients and their families to plan for and cope with the worst. In fact, the document is the first living will that talks about personal, emotional, and spiritual needs as well as medical wishes.

Five Wishes lets your loved one explain exactly how they wish to be treated if they get seriously ill, including things like having their hand held or having relatives pray with them. Five Wishes also provides signees the chance to express their wishes about life support or other medical options as seen in a standard living will. The document is very easy to use—all a person has to do is check a box, circle a direction, or write a few sentences to express any wishes. Five Wishes is produced by Aging with Dignity, a national nonprofit organization with a mission to affirm and safeguard the human dignity of individuals as they age and to promote better care for those near the end of life.

"Death Is Imminent" and Other Conditions

When most people hear that "**death is imminent**," they probably think that death is days or perhaps a week or two away. Not too many people would consider six months to be imminent. However, in medical terms, an "imminent death" means the attending physician determines that death will occur in a relatively short period of time, even if life-sustaining treatment is initiated or continued. One becomes qualified for hospice care if death is imminent, meaning that the person will die within the next six months.

Life-sustaining treatment means any medical treatment, procedure, or intervention that the attending physician believes, when applied to a patient with a qualifying condition, would not be effective to remove the qualifying condition or would serve only to prolong the dying process. Those procedures can include, but are not limited to, assisted ventilation, renal dialysis, surgical procedures, blood transfusions, and the administration of drugs, antibiotics, and artificial nutrition and hydration.

Qualifying conditions are the conditions that cause a living will to come into effect. They typically trigger a doctor to talk to a family member who has a health-care power of attorney about making an end-of-life decision, or cause an attending physician to say no to additional life-sustaining treatment or to make a referral to hospice.

A powerful power of attorney includes language that allows the patient to tell his or her family what to do in such situations, *even though they may not be diagnosed as being terminally ill.* Most living wills and health-care power of attorney forms include instructions regarding life- prolonging treatment. The triggering event for the decision to withhold or withdraw life- prolonging treatment is usually a diagnosis by the principal's attending physician that the principal suffers from a terminal condition, injury, or illness from which death is imminent.

Keep in mind that many physicians do not diagnose either Alzheimer's-type dementia or other dementias as a "terminal condition, injury, or illness from which death is imminent." You may wish to discuss your feelings about life-prolonging treatment with a lawyer when and if your loved one reaches the moderate and/or late stages of dementia.

Real-Life Story: Life-Support Decisions

One afternoon, a man who had been diagnosed with Parkinson's disease entered our law firm office with his wife of many years and a caring adult daughter. We told him that we needed to discuss one of the most difficult questions that a lawyer has to ask a client—we needed to talk about feeding tubes, hydration/water, ventilators, and other life-prolonging treatment. These things are all the more difficult to deal with when looking at a man who has a high probability of being alive, incapable, and subject to the life-and-death decision-making of his loved ones.

We took a breath and then looked into the man's eyes. The man met our gaze, and then we placed a hand over the man's hand and said, "Your family needs to hear from you how you feel about life-prolonging treatment. I understand that you have been diagnosed with Parkinson's disease. One of the things that may happen with Parkinson's is that you may get to the point where you won't be able to make your own life-and-death decisions. You may not actually die from Parkinson's disease—but you have a high probability of dying from a complication of Parkinson's. You may get to the point where the doctor comes to your family and says that you are unable to make a decision about life support, and they must decide whether or not you should have a feeding tube or hydration or a ventilator. What do you want your family to do? Do you want these things?"

The man looked at us, his lawyers, and then he looked at his family. He answered firmly, "I do not want that! Just keep me comfortable."

We turned to his wife and his daughter and asked them if they understood his wishes and if they would be able to make sure that his wishes were respected when other family members show up and insist that "we have to do everything we can for Dad!" They were given a chance to talk, and after that the daughter said, "Dad, I am so grateful that I know what you want. It gives me such peace of mind to be sure about what you would want us to do."

Once your loved one's wishes are clear, it is essential to get them down in writing.

Discussing end-of-life decisions can be difficult, but it will give everyone clarity and peace of mind when these life-support issues arise.

For example, it is very common for doctors to recommend a feeding tube when a person with late-stage dementia is no longer able to swallow. The individual's opinion on life-prolonging treatment when and if they have dementia and need a feeding tube should be added into their health-care power of attorney. That is the sort of customization we mean when we refer to adding a "powerful power" to your power of attorney document.

Another example of a powerful power of attorney is to give a person with dementia the opportunity to say, "You know what? I don't want any curative health care either." Everyone has a constitutional right to refuse medical treatments. If your loved one doesn't put that in their power of attorney, however, they will be given antibiotics or other curative treatments even when they are in late-stage dementia. Don't let that happen to your loved one. Have them create a powerful power of attorney that specifically states their feelings about health care when and if they reach late-stage dementia. The patient should not just hope that no one will prolong his or her life against their will.

You should sit down with your loved one and ask them what kind of treatment they will want if they suffer from dementia. Few people would know that the U.S. health-care system does not define dementia as a terminal illness, even though it ends in death.

This information is incredibly important to every senior who is creating a health-care power of attorney. Tell your lawyer you want a health-care power of attorney that clearly expresses your feelings about health care when and if you have dementia. We guarantee that concept is not a part of traditional planning for health-care powers of attorney. Speak up!

Power of Attorney for Property (Financial Decisions)

You can hire a lawyer to draft a power of attorney for property (financial decisions) to include one or more specific tasks, such as paying bills, or it can be all-encompassing. All-encompassing documents include the authority to cash checks, withdraw funds from bank accounts, pay taxes, trade stock, buy or sell property, take out loans, or take other actions. The all-encompassing document is best for people with Alzheimer's, as long as they have an agent whom they fully trust.

Ask your lawyer about including the following items when drafting the power of attorney for financial decisions:

- the power to apply for public benefits entitlements like Medicaid/ Medi-Cal
- the power to make gifts from the individual to specified loved ones such as a spouse and/or disabled child
- the power to do Medicaid-related asset protection
- the power to remove and/or add assets to a trust, if the individual has a trust

As with health-care powers of attorney, lawyers can draft financial powers of attorney to be "durable," and it is strongly recommended that this be done for people with Alzheimer's disease. A durable power of attorney remains valid and in effect even after your loved one becomes incapacitated.

A durable power of attorney may be drafted to be immediate or "springing", depending on the state law and the time and manner in which the powers become effective. An immediate power of attorney takes effect upon signing—as one would expect. A **springing power of attorney** does not take effect until the principal becomes incapacitated. Generally, durable powers of attorney are effective immediately upon signing and will remain effective after the principal becomes incompetent.

Powerful or Powerless Power of Attorney for Property?

When dealing with a loved one with Alzheimer's, it is a good idea to include the power to gift the interest in a couples' home to the healthy spouse. Unfortunately, that power will not be found in the typical power of attorney for property.

We had a client whose husband had Alzheimer's and was incapacitated. So we looked at their documents; he had previously drafted a traditional power of attorney for property. We looked for a power that said "power to gift my interest in my home to my wife," but it did not exist. It's not in the statutory powers of attorney forms. Even when gifting is mentioned, it's usually limited to tax-related gifting power. Those traditional tax-related gifting powers are insufficient to empower a transfer of the incapacitated principal's interest in the marital residence to their healthy spouse.

46

Without a gifting power that allows nursing-home asset protection within the estate plan, the will and/or trust, and the powers of attorney are totally powerless to help people with long-term care problems. The client is forced to file a guardianship at great expense. The spouse likely has to go before a judge and plead, "Your Honor, please, my husband would have intended for his portion of the home to be transferred to me."

The spouse is going to win 50 percent of the time because the judge agrees that is most likely the case. The other 50 percent of the time the judge is going to say, "No. All of your husband's assets must be used for his health-care needs. If he had wanted to allow you to transfer his interest, then it would have been included within your powers of attorney and estate planning documents."

The nightmare scenario above can be avoided with some careful drafting that can change a powerless power of attorney for property into a powerful one.

What follows is an example of just a few of the powers that help to create a more powerful power of attorney for property. These are powers that people who are in long-term care may need. While there are many family situations in which one would never use the following powers, they may come in handy to the majority of couples with long-term relationships.

1. My agent shall have the power to change beneficiary designations or ownership on life insurance policies, annuities, or individual retirement accounts or other retirement-plan accounts owned by me.

2. My agent shall also have the power to sever any joint tenancies or tenancies by the entirety on my behalf.

3. In addition to the power contained herein, my agent shall have the power to create, alter, amend, fund, or revoke any inter vivos trust, including, but not limited to, any account held as a Totten trust where I am the trustee or cotrustee, and/or to create and fund a special-needs trust to benefit a member of my family.

4. My agent shall have the power to change the ownership of any asset owned by me to my spouse or a trust created for the benefit of my spouse.

5. My agent shall have the power to change the ownership of any assets owned by me to a child of mine who is legally disabled or to a trust for that child's benefit.

These are examples of the types of powers that will make your power of attorney for property powerful. Make sure you talk to your elder law attorney about these powers to ensure your loved one's power of attorney for property is as powerful as it can be. All of these powers are subject to abuse by unscrupulous agents. Seek out highly experienced and reputable elder law attorneys to design safeguards to protect the principal within such documents.

Do Not Resuscitate Order (DNR)

A DNR instructs health-care professionals not to perform cardiopulmonary resuscitation (CPR) if a person's heart stops or the person stops breathing. DNRs are signed by a doctor and put in the individual's medical chart. A DNR, which in some states is the same as a Physician's Order of Life Sustaining Treatment (POLST), is the only document that has sufficient legal authority to stop emergency medical responders from resuscitating an individual.

It is important to know that the DNR is the only advance directive that is also a doctor's order or a physician's order for medical care. It is a two-page document, and the only thing that's important is what's on page one. So, if there's absolutely nothing on page two, but page one is filled out correctly, that's a valid DNR. A photocopy of a DNR is also a valid document.

There are two boxes to check on page one. The first is Full Cardiopulmonary Arrest (when both breathing and heartbeat stop), and the box to be checked is followed by the words, "Do not attempt cardiopulmonary resuscitation (CPR)." The second box is Pre-Arrest Emergency (when breathing is labored or stopped and the heart is still beating). Under this heading is the option to check that a person wants or does not want CPR in this situation.

Many people think that signing a DNR is a substitute for having a valid health-care power of attorney or a living will. That is not the case. The entire scope of the DNR is listed in items one and two. A DNR covers only full cardiopulmonary arrest or pre-arrest emergency. It has nothing to do with any other circumstance as far as dealing with life-prolonging treatment. If a person is in a coma or a vegetative state and wants to die with dignity, a DNR will be powerless to help.

A DNR is not a substitute for a valid health-care power of attorney or even a living will. It is a very specific declaration: "Don't give me treatment if we're dealing with a medical condition called full cardiopulmonary arrest or medical condition called a pre-arrest emergency." It provides no guidance otherwise—none.

The DNR may be invalidated if the immediate cause of a respiratory or cardiac arrest is related to trauma or mechanical airway obstruction. That means if someone has a DNR and is experiencing a respiratory or cardiac arrest, but it turns out that the person is choking on a hot dog, when the EMT shows up and realizes that the person is choking and can't breathe, the EMT will remove that obstruction from the airway. The spouse can wave that DNR in front of the EMT all she wants and the EMT will pay no attention because the person is choking from a traumatic cause, not a chronic condition.

Choosing an Agent

It is important to remember that a person may be able to appoint multiple agents. If you have a loved one in the early stages of Alzheimer's, they may want to appoint one person to have power of attorney for financial matters and another to have power of attorney for health care.

Family members typically act as the agent(s), but some people may chose to ask a close friend to serve as their agent. When picking an agent, it is critical to pick someone honest, trustworthy, capable, and reliable. In order to make certain that your loved one chooses an agent carefully, it is imperative that the agent be on board with the decisions that the principal (your loved one) is making regarding organ donations and life support.

Life support certainly is the crux of a durable power of attorney for health care. There are many examples of cases in which the appointed agent has refused to follow through on the direction provided by the principal. This often involves cases in which the principal does not want life support and the agent is incapable of removing life support. This frequently happens when a parent has appointed a child to serve as agent.

Often, people are pressured to pick a family member, but that family member may not be the right choice for religious, moral, or other reasons. For example, the family member may not be willing to follow the wishes of an individual who wishes to be removed from life support. That is an example of choosing the wrong power of attorney agent.

Sometimes the person named as the agent becomes unable, unavailable, or unwilling to fulfill their duties. Your lawyer should offer to draft a power of attorney with alternate or even multiple agents.

In the case of multiple agents, the documents may be drafted so that they are appointed individually and allowed to act independently. Alternatively, the multiple agents may be appointed jointly so that they are required to act together and come to a consensus. State laws vary.

Real-Life Story: Daughter Can't "Pull the Plug"

We met with our client to discuss her estate plan. Meeting together, we spent close to two hours going over all of the client's wishes relative to her finances, her legacy, and, finally, her views regarding life-prolonging treatments which were incorporated into her health-care power of attorney. The client had been accompanied to this meeting by her daughter, whom she had chosen to be her executor, her trustee, and her agent under her power of attorney for property and health care.

All seemed to be going well until reviewing the client's wishes relative to life-prolonging treatments and end-life decision-making. At that point the daughter suddenly stated, "No, Mom, I could never direct a physician to withhold or remove life support." She was expressing her very strong religious beliefs, as expressed by her church regarding the sanctity of life, and her view of the definition of ordinary health care.

The client was stunned that her daughter would not fulfill her wishes regarding end-life decisions. Certain adjustments needed to be made in the client's health-care decision-making process, and eventually she chose a different person to make the final life-prolonging decision.

It is important to understand not only how a chosen agent may respond to your views on end-life treatment but also the position of the health-care provider. There are many charitable or religious hospitals and nursing homes that will not fulfill your loved one's desires relative to end-life decision-making. In the event that a health-care provider is unwilling to comply with the legitimate end-life decision-making elected by your loved one, you, under the health-care power of attorney, should request that your loved one be moved to a different facility that is willing to fulfill his or her wishes relative to end-of-life decisions.

Physician's Order for Life Sustaining Treatment (POLST)

Physician Orders for Life-Sustaining Treatment (POLST) programs were developed in response to a health-care system that is increasingly overlooking a patient's wishes in favor of other priorities. POLST programs provide a platform for end-of-life conversations between doctors and patients and a uniform way to document the patients' wishes so that patients' desires are understood and prioritized correctly. POLSTs are designed to improve people's quality of care at the end of their lives through the effective communication of their desires and the comprehensive documentation of medical directives.

Expert View: Surprising Truths within Hospice Care

Carolyn Peterson is an RN who has worked as a nurse for 43 years. Seventeen years ago, she began to focus exclusively in the area of hospice care. She works for an organization that provides care for the dying and incurably ill.

Q: You have the capability of working in almost any area of medical care. What attracts you and keeps you working with hospice?

A: I think it's the humanity of the work. We enter a person's life at a time when the rest of the medical community seems to have abandoned them. When people get to the point in their illness where it can't be fixed, a lot of the medical community kind of give up on them. Many times, when I first meet a patient or family, I might be the first one to have explained what's going on in terms of their disease and that; truthfully, there is no more treatment available except hospice. It takes quite a bit of finesse and compassion, and when you have these conversations there are no do-overs.

Q: Please explain the composition of a hospice team.

A: Medicare dictates who must be a part of the interdisciplinary hospice team. The top person is the medical director, who is an employee of the hospice and must be a doctor who is board cer-tified in hospice and palliative care (relieving and preventing suf-fering). There must be a nurse case manager, a nondenominational chaplain, and a social worker.

Q: In a typical month, how many different patients or clients are cared for by a team?

A: Many hospice teams service 12 to 13 new families per month.

Q: What are the typical services that one could expect to find pro-vided by hospice on a per-day basis, and who pays for it?

A: Medicare Part A pays for hospice care at 100 percent. It does not require any supplemental insurance, because the Medicare hos-pice benefit covers it. Medicare provides for four different lev-els of hospice care. Some companies provide all four levels of care even though two of the levels can be financially risky (not profitable).

Q: Could you clarify the four different levels of care?

A: The very basic level of care is called "routine level of care." That's the absolute minimum that Medicare expects a hospice to do. And that is where a patient can be seen anywhere from daily to every 14 days by the nurse, a certified nursing assistant, the chaplain, or a social worker. That's the very basic level of care.

The next level is called "respite care." Normally, seniors don't qualify for skilled nursing care unless they've been in an acute-care hospital for at least 72 hours. The exception to that is hospice, for a patient living at home when the person caring for them becomes injured or sick or perhaps there's a fire in the house. The hospice will pay for that patient to be transferred to a nursing home and we will pay for five nights at that facility while we sort out the situation. Or let's say they're living at home with a daughter or son who needs a break. We can bring the person to a nursing home, and that's one of the rare times that Medicare will pay for nursing home care without that initial acute hospitalization stay.

The third level of care is "continuous care" or "comfort care." This is the most financially risky area of care for the agency. It enables us to put a nurse at the bedside to manage pain symptoms and end-of-life care. There are very specific criteria—certain combinations of nursing home hours versus CNA [certified nurse assistant] hours. There are only so many hours per every 24 that a patient receives care in order for the agency to be reimbursed. If you're off by even 15 minutes, you may not get paid. But we provide that level of care because it enables our patients to die at home. We are one of the few agencies that do that.

The highest level of care is called "general inpatient care." That is done in a facility where there's a registered nurse on the premises at all times—a Medicare-accredited hospital setting or skilled nursing facility. It's the only time that Medicare allows the hospice to pay room and board in a skilled area. There are very specific criteria to qualify. An example would be somebody at home who is not doing well, but they would like to be around when their grandson comes home from college for a final goodbye. The decision might be made to take them to a hospital or nursing home to start an IV to get some hydration going and help make that wish come true.

So those are the four levels of care. All hospices do the routine level of care. Most will do respite care because there's no financial risk involved. There are very few hospital-based hospices that do all four levels.

Q: If you think about the top three causes of death, what would those be?

A: Untreatable cancer would be right up there. End-stage dementia, where the patient has reached the point where the brain is no longer telling them that they're hungry or thirsty, or where they're not swallowing correctly, would be another. And lastly, with seniors, adult failure to thrive. Due to old age, a person's body is not utilizing the nutrition it's taking in and they're losing weight and just not thriving. And after that would be congestive heart failure and chronic obstructive pulmonary disease.

Q: How long does hospice care last?

A: Medicare is a six-month benefit, but as long as the person and hospice meet the criteria, that can be extended. And again, that's a financial risk that the hospice takes because there is a cap. A good hospice will keep you past six months if you still meet the criteria for whatever illness you've been admitted under.

Q: Who makes the decision about whether or not someone's still qualified?

A: Medicare insists on two doctors to certify that somebody has a prognosis of six months or less to live. Typically, those two doctors are the attending physician and the medical director of the hospice. It's called the certificate of terminal illness.

Q: Talk to me about end-stage dementia and a person's not being able to take hydration—death by dehydration.

A: When people get to the point where they're not eating or drinking on their own, it's usually because something is going on in their brain, whether it's advanced dementia, aggressive cancer, or a lack of oxygen because of congestive heart failure or a lung condition. You or I would feel hunger pains and we would feel thirsty. People at that stage don't. As they become dehydrated, they get weak and sleepy. The kidneys are starting to shut down from lack of hydration. The individual goes into a coma, and from that coma they pass away. It's truly that simple. Hospice does not mean accelerating the death process.

CHAPTER 5

MEDICARE

This is a quote from President Lyndon B. Johnson at the time of his signing the Medicare and Medicaid bill on July 30, 1965:

> No longer will older Americans be denied the healing miracle of modern medicine. No longer will illness crush and destroy the savings that they have so carefully put away over a lifetime so that they might enjoy dignity in their later years. No longer will young families see their own incomes, and their own hopes, eaten away simply because they are carrying out their moral obligations to their parents, and to their uncles and aunts. And no longer will this nation refuse the hand of justice to those who have given a lifetime of service and wisdom and labor to the progress of this progressive country.

President Johnson spoke those words during the ceremonial signing of the Medicaid-Medicare Act in 1965. Medicare was just part of an enormous sea of change of domestic programs (which he had named the "Great Society") which were intended to eliminate poverty and inequity in the United States.

Medicare was created to ensure that United States citizens who had reached the age of 65 would have access to affordable medical services. On the other hand, **Medicaid/Medi-Cal** was created with a different platform; it was designed as a poverty program which now provides benefits to impoverished seniors, children, and other low-income citizens and residents of the United States.

The world of 1965 was a far different world than 2018 and beyond. For those of us who were alive in 1965, among the most popular bands were the Rolling Stones, the Beatles, the Beach Boys, and the Supremes.

Many of us who were alive at that time paid little note to the creation of Medicare and Medicaid. Now, no senior citizen in America would tolerate the elimination of this important public health-care benefit.

The foundations of Medicare were designed for a 1965 health-care world. Medicare was designed to pay for medical treatment for the five big killers of senior citizens:

1. Heart attack

2. Stroke

3. Infectious diseases

4. Cancer

5. Agricultural and industrial accidents

All of those killers still exist—but life expectancies have been greatly extended. In 1965, the average life expectancy for American men was 66 years and 73 years for women. Recently in a front-page article of the *Wall Street Journal*, it was stated that the *majority* of 65-year-old men will now live to be nearly 85. Most women will outlive men by five to seven years—achieving a life expectancy that is now beyond 90 years of age. *Medicare was not designed to deal with the long-term health-care issues of frail and old/old octogenarian seniors. Medicare does not cover long-term-care expenses!*

The good news of this lengthening life expectancy carries its own inherent problems. Medicare was created to pay for acute health problems. Medicare reimbursement is based on repayment according to the Center for Medicare & Medicaid Services (CMS) reimbursement coding policies and coding conventions, as defined in the American Medical Association's Current Procedural Terminology (CPT) manual. Medicare does not have reimbursement codes for the major cost components of long-term care. Those who need long-term care need non- medical assistance which begins in the home, progresses to the assisted living facility, and then eventually ends at a skilled nursing facility, a/k/a nursing home.

Medicare will continue to pay for acute-care health issues throughout the life of the senior. But Medicare was never designed to be a provider of health care at home, in an assisted living facility, or in a nursing home. So with the coming of this new age of longevity, our seniors' life spans have exceeded the coverage of Medicare.

Medicare is a wonderful program—*except* for seniors who are on the long-term care path. Where *Medicare* stops, no governmental care is provided unless and until the person is so impoverished that they qualify for the state/federal hybrid known as *Medicaid*, except in California the program is called Medi-Cal. (A discussion of Medicaid is in Chapter 6.)

When it comes down to it, the health-care system isn't a whole lot different from a lottery system. If someone gets a diagnosis for which there is a Medicare reimbursement code, then "Medicare cares" about that person's care and will cover it. If someone has needs that are not listed within the Medicare Reimbursement Codes, then that need is not covered by Medicare, Medicare does *not* care about that person's specific care, and that person will have to spend their own until that have reach the 'limited resources' standard for nursing home Medicaid or in California, Medi-Cal.

Real-Life Story: Two Sisters

There's a story of two sisters of the same relative age, sharing the same genes and even living on the same street. One sister had heart issues and diabetes and was able to rely on Medicare. The other sister was not so lucky and had Alzheimer's disease, and was unable to qualify for Medicare to pay for her in-home; assisted living and nursing home care needs. In essence, the first sister won the diagnosis lottery!

Medicare cares about helping seniors to recover from heart attacks or strokes and other acute-care health issues. For the sister who had diabetes and a resulting heart problem, there are Medicare reimbursement codes to take care of almost everything she needed: medication, health services, rehab services, hospital services, doctor services. . . She was provided with an enormous amount of care—probably half a million dollars or more—because there was a Medicare reimbursement code for her diagnosis.

Medicare didn't completely abandon the sister with Alzheimer's. When she got a urinary tract infection (UTI) and had to go to the hospital as an inpatient, Medicare paid for her acute care. Part B paid for doctor services. Part D helped pay for medications, such as Aricept and Risperdal.

But look at what's not covered! Someone who has memory issues and starts to need assistance will not be able to access Medicare benefits for care. As the sister with Alzheimer's started to have memory issues, she was still living at home. One day she decided to turn on the water in the bathtub

---

(continued on next page)

upstairs, and she didn't turn it off. . . She didn't turn it off for a couple of days! At this point it became obvious that she was no longer safe in a normal environment and somebody needed to be overseeing her activities of daily living. She needed in-home care.

Medicare does not care about in-home care or assisted-living care or nursing home care. There are no Medicare reimbursement codes for that type of care. The sister diagnosed with Alzheimer's started to have memory issues that caused her to be unsafe in her own environment, and she needed to have someone come in to be with her, or she needed to go somewhere where she would be supervised and the environment was safe and controlled, Medicare does not care about providing that kind of care.

That means that the sister with Alzheimer's will have to pay for her care out of her pocket—out of her savings account. If she had a long-term-care policy, it may have helped pay for Alzheimer's care. With a long-term care policy, Medicare still continues to pay for all the things that it paid for before: acute care.

The sister with Alzheimer's must pay for care at home. When she finally gets down to $2,000 or less of total assets (because she's a single person), she can then qualify for Medicaid nursing home benefits and she can move to a nursing home.

Up the street, her sister with diabetes and heart problems has had over $500,000 of health care provided by Medicare and hasn't had to spend down all of her assets.

Today, it's common that people don't like the fact that someone is helping seniors qualify for Medicaid, because Medicaid is using government money. However, think of it this way: The first sister didn't do anything wrong. She had a heart attack and the government happily paid for her benefits. But the second sister worked all of her life, saved her money, and also did everything right. Why should she be denied care?

When Medicare was created in 1965, it was designed to cover "**acute care**" because those were the common issues of the time. Strokes, heart attacks, and cancer were the big health issues. Now a couple of generations have passed, and the problems of the elderly are no longer confined to acute-care issues. ("Acute care" is defined as short-term treatment for a condition or illness from which recovery is expected.)

Many seniors believe that Medicare will pay for their nursing home costs. After all, the language states that Medicare will pay for "**skilled care**," and we refer to facilities as independent, assisted, and skilled. Many seniors are shocked to discover that the benefits they paid into will *not* pay for "skilled care" in a nursing home.

To-Do Checklist

❑ Understand the difference between Medicare and Medicaid.

❑ Understand the limitations of Medicare as it applies to Alzheimer's disease.

❑ Know the eligibility rules for Medicaid (see Chapter 6).

❑ Know what assets are exempt under Medicaid (see Chapter 6).

❑ Know what benefits veterans and their families are entitled to, and how to claim them (see Chapter 8).

Medicare Contrasted with Medicaid/Medi-Cal

Medicare is the federal medical insurance plan for senior citizens and individuals with disabilities, but the program does not cover the kind of long-term care that those afflicted with Alzheimer's disease require.

Medicare provides care for individuals over the age of 65, blind, or with disabilities who need "**acute medical care**." That means it provides care for those senior citizens who have been diagnosed with an illness or other medical issue where there is a high probability that the patient can recover and return to a normal life. You do not recover from Alzheimer's disease. Acute care is the opposite of chronic or long-term care.

When Medicare was created in 1965, the average male died before reaching 67 years of age and the average female lived to be about 73. So when Medicare was first designed, it was created in a society where many people would never qualify for it or, if they did qualify, they would qualify for a relatively short amount of time. But times have changed!

Many people believe that Medicaid is only about paying for care for poor people. Medicaid was designed to be that part of the social safety net that provided health care for people who were too poor to have their own health care. It was limited in what it was going to do because it was **"means tested"**—in other words, it is available only if someone qualifies for certain poverty limitations.

In 1965 there was no such thing as assisted living facilities. Assisted living is for a person that has gotten to the point in life of having **"chronic care"** conditions—"chronic" meaning that the person is never going to get well. That is an important difference between Medicare and Medicaid. When you have Alzheimer's disease, you are not going to get well.

Medicare does not usually cover chronic medical care services for individuals who are suffering from a long-term illness or medical problem where there is a high probability that they will not recover and will not return to a normal life.

Many people believe that Medicare will provide them with long-term care benefits if they need to be in an assisted living facility or a nursing home—but unfortunately, they are mistaken.

Medicare: A Closer Look

Let's take a closer look at Medicare. As we noted above, Medicare is primarily designed to provide care for people over the age of 65 who need medical care, but will get well. Medicare is supposed to pay for acute care assuming the person needing the care is placed as an inpatient.

Medicare does not care about Alzheimer's disease. Medicare was never designed for long-term care.

Although Medicare can sometimes cover up to 100 days in a skilled nursing facility, it is intended for patients who need recovery or rehabilitation services after a surgery or illness. For Medicare to pay for a stay in a nursing home, patients must *continue to recover* during their stay.

Individuals in the middle to late stages of Alzheimer's require **custodial care** instead of rehabilitative care. "Custodial care" means assistance with preparing meals, bathing, grooming, toileting, and other activities of normal daily life. It seems like custodial care is a skilled type of care and it even involves measures to keep individuals from harming themselves or others—but Medicare is not going to pay for this custodial care.

Medicare Coverage and Deductibles

There are four parts of Medicare coverage: hospital insurance (Part A), medical insurance (Part B), Medicare advantage plans, and Medicare prescription drug plans (Plan D), all with their own eligibility requirements.

Hospital Insurance (Part A): Inpatient Hospital Services; Skilled Nursing Services (Rehab Services); Home Agency Services and Hospice Services

Most people age 65 or older who are citizens or permanent residents of the United States are eligible for free Medicare hospital insurance (Part A). Part A helps pay for inpatient rehabilitation care in a hospital or skilled-nursing facility (following a hospital stay), some home health care, and hospice care. Medicare covers 100 percent of medically necessary home health-care services, but the individual pays 20 percent of the cost for medical equipment. Part A hospital inpatient deductible varies per year and the most current information can be found at www.medicare.gov. In 2018, the deductible to be paid by the Medicare recipient-patient is $1,340 for each benefit period (spell of illness) and additional costs per day after the 60th day of any hospital stay. There is a lifetime maximum benefit.

Medicare covers **hospice care**. To qualify for hospice care, a doctor must certify that an individual is terminally ill with six months or less to live. Coverage here includes drugs and medical costs, including equipment and services. Medicare usually does not cover things like spiritual and grief counseling. An individual pays nothing for hospice care, but does pay up to $5 per prescription for outpatient drugs and 5 percent of the costs for inpatient respite care.

Medical Insurance (Part B): Position and other Professional Services; Outpatient Hospital including Outpatient Hospital Observation Stays; Outpatient Lab & X Ray; Other Therapy Services; and Durable Medical Equipment

Anyone who is eligible for free Medicare hospital insurance (Part A) can enroll in Medicare medical insurance (Part B) by paying a monthly premium. An individual who is not eligible for free hospital insurance can buy medical insurance, without having to buy hospital insurance, if that person is age 65 or older and is:

- a U.S. citizen or
- a lawfully admitted noncitizen who has lived in the U.S. for at least five years.

Part B helps pay for doctor services and many other medical services and supplies that are not covered by hospital insurance.

Under Medicare, if the Part B deductible applies, a person must pay all costs until meeting the yearly Part B deductible (first $183 per year of Part B medical expenses and then 20 percent of the Medicare approved amount for most doctor services including those which are received in the hospital; outpatient therapy; and durable medical equipment) before Medicare begins to pay its share. After the deductible is met, the person typically pays 20 percent of the Medicare-approved amount of the service, if the doctor or other health-care provider accepts assignment. There is no yearly limit for what a person pays out-of-pocket.

Medicare Prescription Drug Plans (Part D): Prescription Drugs. (Patient purchases this separately from selected insurance companies for additional premium paid to insurance company)

Part D helps pay for medications doctors prescribe for treatment. Anyone who has Medicare hospital insurance (Part A), medical insurance (Part B) or a Medicare Advantage plan (Part C) is eligible for prescription drug coverage (Part D). Joining a Medicare prescription drug plan is voluntary, and it requires an additional monthly premium. Some beneficiaries with higher incomes will pay a higher monthly Part D premium. The Part D premium varies due to the cost of the Prescription Drug Plan (PDP) which will provide the specific drugs which are required by each specific Medicaid recipient. Deductibles vary wildly and are unpredictable due the cost of differing medications. The fastest growing cost of health care is medications.

Medigap Policies

Medicare supplement insurance fills the "gaps" between Medicare benefits and what a person must pay out-of-pocket for deductibles, coinsurance, and copayments. Medigap policies are sold by private insurance companies that are typically licensed and regulated by their state Department of Insurance. These policies pay only for services that Medicare deems as medically necessary, and payments are generally based on the Medicare-approved charge. Some plans offer benefits that Medicare does not, such as emergency care while in a foreign country.

Medicare Advantage Plans (Part C)

Individuals who have Medicare Parts A and B can join a Medicare Advantage plan. Although, Medicare Advantage plans are listed as Medicare Part C, in fact, every Medicare Advantage member is unenrolled from Medicare coverage. Medicare Advantage plans are insurance company contracts and not direct governmental benefits. You must read and understand the actual contract to determine what benefits are actually being promised by the Medicare Advantage plans. All of the plans are offered by private companies and approved by Medicare. Medicare Advantage plans generally cover many of the same benefits that a **Medigap policy** (discussed above) would cover, such as extra days in the hospital after having used the number of days that Medicare covers.

Part C plans are available in many areas. People with Medicare Parts A and B can choose to receive all of their health-care services through one of these provider organizations under Part C. Consumer advocates such as the Center for Medicare and Medicaid Advocacy, www.medicareadvocacy.org have filed numerous complaints with the federal government which allege that many insurance company's Medicare Advantage Plans fail to fulfill their promises.

Please do online investigation of specific Medicare Advantage plans before purchase. In addition, it is critically important that you verify with your preferred hospital and doctors that they are in the network of your prospective Medicare Advantage plan.

Medicare and Nursing Home Medicaid/Medi-Cal

Now that you better understand Medicare's benefits and limits, please read the chapter on Nursing Home Medicaid. Most persons affected by Alzheimer's Disease will need to qualify for both of those governmental benefits to be able to pay for their medical needs. If your loved one is a wartime veteran, please also read the chapter on wartime veterans' benefits.

CHAPTER 6
NURSING HOME MEDICAID/MEDI-CAL

In California, Medi-Cal, and in other states, Medicaid pays nursing home costs for certain qualified individuals. We shall refer to both nursing home Medicaid and Medi-Cal by using only the term Medicaid. In a few cases, it covers very limited home- and community-based health-care services, such as assistance with bathing, light housekeeping, cooking, and laundry, while a "qualified individual" remains at home. But the predominant use of nursing home Medicaid is the pay for long-term care expenses once a person has run out of money and out of other options.

The federal government provides a matching grant to each state to cover approximately 50 percent to 80 percent of the program costs within the state, and the state pays the rest. As we frequently hear in the news, both the federal government and our state government often spend more than they take in and Medicaid seems to be one of the places that they always try to cut. After all, it's easy to make cuts to Medicaid because, from many people's point of view, it's not a "necessary" benefit.

The truth for the majority of US citizens is that nursing home Medicaid is an absolutely necessary benefit. These days the monthly cost for a nursing home typically ranges between $5,000 and $10,000 per month, and seniors who worked for decades often have only enough savings to pay for just a few months of full-time long-term care costs in a nursing home.

Many people think about Medicaid with disdain, but it is not a moral failure to need assistance with long-term care when you have a long-term care illness with extraordinarily high costs. Our country made a political decision that Medicare would provide care for seniors based on the type of disease or infirmity they have, almost without regard to cost. If you have the right diagnosis, Medicare will take care of your doctor bills, your hospital costs, and your rehab expenses.

On the other hand, Medicare was not designed to pay for the kind of care needed if you have the misfortune of having dementia or other long-term care needs. You are on your own to pay for your care at home; in assisted living facility; and/or in a nursing home.

Nursing home Medicaid does not come to your rescue unless and until you are sufficiently broke. The government uses a fancier term than "broke;" their words are "limited resources."

This chapter is designed to teach you how nursing home Medicaid can rescue many individuals who desperately need long-term care. With proper planning, you can pay what the law requires to become eligible for nursing home Medicaid, but not one penny more. This may be the most important chapter of this book. So what exactly is nursing home Medicaid?

Medicaid is a joint program between the federal government and the individual states. Therefore, its implementation in each state is markedly different, because the actual Medicaid rules are created by the state (and reviewed by the federal government to ensure that the states don't violate the federal rules). Individual states do have substantial leeway to modify the application of Medicaid within their borders. It is important to find a qualified attorney within the state in which one is seeking to qualify for nursing home Medicaid benefits.

Medicaid was created by the same law that created Medicare, but unlike Medicare, one must meet the limited income and resources rules of each state to access the benefits of Medicaid. Those limitations are described as **"means test testing."** In other words, if a person has sufficient means as defined by the government, then that person does not qualify for Medicaid.

Medicaid was built on a public aid model and if one does not meet the strict income and resource rules then, regardless of a person's medical needs, no benefits shall be paid.

As discussed in the prior chapter, Medicare is focused on hospital care and rehabilitation. Medicaid provides those benefits and nursing home care and personal care services. This chapter will focus on nursing home Medicaid, which is only a portion of the benefits that are available to persons of all ages whose income and resources are insufficient to pay for health care. To obtain Medicaid, one must be a US citizen or legal permanent resident.

Real-Life Story: The Dangers of Not Being Familiar with Nursing Home Medicaid Rules

One of the authors notes, "I would never want to disparage another lawyer, but sometimes I am appalled at what I hear from a client who received really bad advice from their family lawyer."

The author had one such client whose father was in the late stages of Parkinson's disease. The client had a very capable estate planning attorney work with her parents to create their estate plan. When the estate planning documents had been prepared and signed (and the plan was simply "sweetheart planning." It essentially stated, "If I die, you take everything, Sweetheart. Same goes for me."), one of the four daughters turned to their family lawyer and said, "What if my dad needs to go to a nursing home?" To which the lawyer replied, "You don't want to put your dad in a nursing home."

Most people don't want to put a loved one in a nursing home, but many times it cannot be avoided. Needless to say, this daughter was quite upset when she found out that there was definitely other (and better) planning that could be done. When the family lawyer called the author's firm wondering why his clients were so upset with him, and the author mentioned the nursing home Medicaid program and the possible need for that program, the family lawyer said, "I don't know anything about nursing home Medicaid." The author replied, "That's what you should have told your clients in the first place."

The author points out that he has never received a call from an estate planner who said, "I'm doing an estate plan and I would like to make sure that I'm not doing anything to violate the Medicaid rules." That conversation has never occurred. However, he has seen the aftermath of mistakes made and the problems those mistakes created for people who later needed these benefits. These are mistakes that would have been avoided had the lawyers known their state's Medicaid rules—or sought advice from a lawyer who did.

To-Do Checklist

❑   Understand the difference between Medicare and Medicaid

❑   Understand the nursing home Medicaid rules

❑   Know the eligibility rules for Medicaid

❏ Know what assets are exempt under Medicaid

❏ Understand how to properly spend down

❏ Learn the nursing home Medicaid myths and how to avoid big money mistakes

❏ Know what benefits veterans and their families are entitled to, and how to claim them (see Chapter 8).

Many people believe that Medicaid is only for the poorest members of our society and therefore, they will never use Medicaid. There is a stigma attached to Medicaid in many people's minds because of this nearly universal belief. However, in the fight against Alzheimer's disease, Medicaid is a very important program, and you should be aware of how it works.

Real-Life Story: The Mythology of Medicaid

A former state senator who had been a very successful accountant and had dealt with senior issues for years told one of the authors, "I don't quite understand what Medicaid has to do with senior citizens."

The author said, "In our state and in the U.S. in general, the average senior citizen does not have enough personal resources to pay privately for even one year of long-term care services out-of-pocket. Therefore, almost every senior citizen's family who winds up with a loved one requiring long-term care will need to deal with Illinois' Medicaid nursing home benefit qualification rules. That's what Medicaid has to do with senior citizens."

This politician was a very capable person who had been voting on senior issues for over 20 years. But even as a politician, he had no idea that the words "senior citizen" and "Medicaid" applied to each other at any point.

The former senator is not alone in his thinking. This is an example of how few people understand nursing home Medicaid. Unfortunately, the federal government is not working very hard to break this myth. People assume that Medicare will provide care from age 65 to the grave, and that is simply not true.

Medicaid is a "**means-tested entitlement program**" that provides medical benefits to eligible individuals. That means that you must qualify for certain poverty limitations to use Medicaid. The federal government gives grants to the states, covering about 50-80 percent of the program costs, and the state pays the balance. Each state adopts its own rules (within the federal guidelines) for administering the program.

Medicaid pays for nursing home costs for qualified individuals. It can also cover home- and community-based services such as assistance with bathing, light housekeeping, cooking, and laundry while an eligible patient with Alzheimer's remains at home, if a state offers these community programs.

Real-Life Story: Burden on the Caregiving Spouse

An often-overlooked aspect of Alzheimer's disease is the burden placed on caregiving spouses, who often later need care themselves.

One of the book's authors had a client whose husband had Alzheimer's disease and eventually needed long-term care beyond what his wife could provide. Despite the husband's macho declaration that he would put a gun to his head before ever going to a nursing home, the sad truth is that his wife would be the one to bear the burden caused by his long-term care needs and her own aging challenges.

The husband and wife in this example are frugal people who worked hard all their lives. They live on two Social Security checks, his modest pension, and minimal investments. They were able to pay their bills and enjoy simple luxuries—until the out-of-pocket expenses of long-term care begin to drain what they worked a lifetime to save.

The wife selflessly provides in-home care for her beloved husband, but eventually the day will come when her strength is not enough to pick him up or keep him from wandering away from home. On that day, it might be a doctor, a discharge planner, or a police officer who looks into her eyes and speaks the harsh truth: "I'm sorry, ma'am. You can't take care of him by yourself anymore."

(continued on next page)

This poor woman will then face a nightmare as she walks the elder care journey with a frail and declining husband. First, she will learn that neither Medicare nor their health insurance provides any payment for home health-care costs. Later, when her husband must be relocated to a long-term care facility, she will discover that neither Medicare nor Medicare supplemental insurance will pay the facility's $3,000 to $8,000 monthly cost.

Quickly, she also will discover that Medicaid is not available because she has "too much money." Her husband's care will be offset by Medicaid only if she and her husband meet stringent income and asset limitations. If they have assets over $109,560, they will be forced to "spend down" their life savings, which Medicaid defines as "excess assets." When all excess assets have been spent on her husband's medical care, then Medicaid will also control her monthly income. In Illinois, she will be restricted to $2,739 per month from the couple's joint income. If she has more income than this of her own, not counting her husband's income, the state (again in Illinois) will seek a support amount from her to contribute to the payment of his care. (Rules vary among the states.)

Later, when her husband dies, she will receive more bad news. She may lose all or half of his pension, and as the "survivor spouse," she loses one of their two Social Security checks. She has spent nearly all of their assets to provide for her husband's care, and now she can't even afford to live in her own home. The nightmare of long-term care will leave her impoverished and will steal her independence after she has spent many years providing for her husband's care.

She will not have the luxury of a spouse who will serve her as she served him. No one will be there to dutifully care for her at home and to delay the day that she must move to a long-term care facility. She will not have the financial resources that he had, because Medicaid called them "excess nonexempt assets" and she had to spend those assets paying for her husband's care. As a single person, she will not be provided with assistance by the Medicaid system until she has become impoverished to the point of a paltry $2,000 or less in total assets. The indignity committed against her does not stop there, for now she must sign over all her income to the nursing home as well, except for a miserly personal-needs allowance of $30 per month. Not enough to get her hair done, much less to pay for personal items and replace clothing that is worn or that does not come back from the laundry at the nursing home.

The loving wife who faithfully cared for her husband is now out of money and out of options. She is alone—and living the nightmare of long-term care in America.

Nursing Home Medicaid Eligibility

You should be aware that Medicaid eligibility is based on the applicant's medical condition and assets and income. For example, an individual must either live in a nursing home or have a medical need (such as Alzheimer's) that requires nursing home care, to apply for Medicaid to cover residential long-term care costs.

Your loved one will need a medical assessment to establish medical eligibility in order to identify the long-term health-care needs.

It is also necessary to be a U.S. citizen or to be lawfully admitted for permanent residence in the United States. Individuals are required to live in the state where they apply for Medicaid and must intend to make that state their home.

Medicaid strictly limits the assets people may own while accepting benefits. The asset limits are substantially different depending upon whether the Nursing Home Medicaid applicant is single (never-married, divorced, widow, or widower). For an example see chart at end of this chapter.

Nursing Home Medicaid divides assets into three different categories:

1. Exempt Assets
2. Countable Assets
3. Legally Unavailable Assets

While each state has its own limits and its own **exempt assets**, the following are generally exempt assets that do not count against the beneficiary:

- the principal place of residence, subject to restrictions
- household and personal belongings
- one car
- burial plot/prepaid funeral plan
- cash value of permanent life insurance policies up to $1,500
- a small amount of cash (this varies from state to state, but typically a single Medicaid applicant may keep about $2,000 while married couples who both require Medicaid may keep a higher amount)

All other assets are "**countable assets**" and count toward the state-determined maximum income level. Countable assets are bank accounts, CDs, money market accounts, stocks, mutual funds, bonds, retirement accounts, pensions, second cars, second or vacation homes, and any other item that can be valued and turned into cash. Countable assets are also referred to as **available assets.** The concept is that whichever assets are available to you that exceed the exempt assets limits noted above, must be used to pay for your and/or your loved ones health-care needs before you may be eligible to receive Nursing Home Medicaid benefits.

Legally unavailable assets are assets that you do not have the legal power to liquidate. Examples include minority interests in businesses and certain irrevocable trusts.

Principal Place of Residence

In situations where there is a "**community spouse**" (the healthy spouse still living at home), the home is considered an exempt asset. In many states, the community spouse could continue to keep a home of any value. In other words, the community spouse does not have to sell the home to qualify the spouse for Medicaid.

You should be aware, though, that some states place a limit on the equity value that a person can have in a home. These limits typically range from $750,000 to $5 million of equity that a person can have in a home or else be forced to sell it.

In many states if a person is a *single individual* and goes into a nursing home, it is assumed that the person is not returning to their home. Therefore, the state will require that the home be listed for sale if the person has not returned to the home after 120 days. That person can claim what is called an "intent to return" and not have to sell the home, but some states will place a lien against the house, and the lien is based on whatever the eventual total amount of Medicaid that is expended on that person's behalf—so that when that house is sold, the state has a claim against the proceeds.

You also need to be aware of the rules in your state regarding liens placed against the home. In some states, although the home is "exempt," the state stands ready to file a lien for the amount paid toward the institutionalized spouse at the time the community spouse passes away.

Community Spouse Resource Allowance (CSRA)

What happens when a couple's countable assets are *above* the countable asset or **Community Spouse Resource Allowance** (CSRA)?

When one spouse has a disease like Alzheimer's and needs Medicaid assistance, but the other spouse is still healthy, the couple is faced with dividing their assets. The federal government allows the states to choose levels of exempt assets within a range of what's allowed under the federal standards. These exempt assets are called the "**community spouse resource allowance**" (**CSRA**). This will be the amount of money available to a community spouse as a resource allowance when an institutionalized spouse applies for benefits under the Medicaid program.

Most states require you to fully disclose all assets owned either jointly or individually by either spouse.

A couple's countable assets are calculated as of the date that the institutionalized spouse is placed in a Medicaid-certified bed. Typically this date, or the "**snapshot date**," is the date that the spouse enters a hospital or nursing home for a continuous stay of at least 30 days.

Thus, a couple would add up all of their countable assets as they stand on their snapshot date and divide by two. The community spouse is entitled to keep half, up to the federal maximum. For example, the federal maximum CSRA for 2017 was $120,900, but the federal government allows the states to set the CSRA as low as a minimum of $24,180.

It is very important to understand that the state calculates what the community spouse can keep. Although it could be as much as $120,900, it can be much less. Furthermore, the institutionalized spouse (the spouse in the nursing home) can have as much as $2,000 in countable assets in some jurisdictions, or it may be much less.

Allowable Spousal Income, or the Minimum Monthly Maintenance Needs Allowance (MMMNA)

When one spouse needs nursing home services to be paid for by the state through the Medicaid program, there is a limit to the allowable income for the community spouse. If the community spouse has income of their own, they need to be aware of their state's **Minimum Monthly Mainte-nance Needs Allowance (MMMNA)**. Income above the allowable limit is allocated to the cost of the nursing home spouse's care. The amount of allocation varies per state and is an area in which an experienced elder law attorney can provide valuable advice.

CRSA Asset Example and Spend Down:

First, let's look at the "exempt assets." A couple has a house that is valued at approximately $300,000 and two vehicles. In some states, the community spouse can have one vehicle of any value and the institutionalized spouse can have a vehicle as long as the value is not more than $4,500 (unless it is a special vehicle for transportation due to medical needs—i.e., a wheelchair van). So, for this example, their house and cars are exempt.

In addition to the house and the cars, they have an annuity of $100,000 that is non-qualified and held jointly, they have a couple of CDs of $20,000 each, a brokerage account of $50,000, and a checking and savings account of about $15,000 total.

In their situation, under the CSRA of their state, the community spouse can protect $109,560 and the institutionalized spouse can have a maximum asset amount of $2,000. Anything over the $111,560, regardless of the type of asset (even IRAs), must be spent down before the institutionalized spouse can qualify for Medicaid.

Your lawyer can apply the same spend-down strategies to the couple as to the single individual so they can pay down any debt. They have an equity line on the house that they used to put on a new roof and siding last year. They owe $30,000 on that, so the lawyers advise them to pay that off. They have credit card debt of $10,000; they pay off that debt. Two prepaid funerals of $15,000 each can be part of the spend-down.

The couple just spent $70,000 to benefit themselves. They are now about $24,500 above the allowable assets. Now they could upgrade the main exempt vehicle. They might need a new furnace or a new mattress or landscaping. They are allowed to pay the attorney legal fees for helping them with this difficult process of long-term care planning. Now they are eligible for Medicaid, and the community spouse is better protected for the future.

For example, in 2018, the MMMNA can be as high as $3,090 before taxes per month. On the other hand, the federal lower limit for MMMNA is $2,030 before taxes per month. The best way to describe this MMMNA is that the state does two levels of testing to determine whether or not there would be some sort of diversion of the institutionalized spouse's income to the healthy community spouse. Following are two examples to illustrate this point.

MMMNA Example No. 1—Alone and Making Adjustments:

The husband has a Social Security check of $1,200 per month and a pension from Ford Motor Company for another $1,200 a month. The wife has a Social Security check of $600 a month.

The husband is getting $2,400 a month. The only income that's coming to the wife in her name is the $600 social security check. Now the husband needs to apply for Medicaid nursing home benefits, because he has Alzheimer's. In the example state, the amount of money he can keep to spend on himself is $30 per month, as a personal-needs allowance. The only other deduction from income for the husband is what he pays for supplemental insurance.

Let us assume that the husband pays $220 for his Medicare supplement (the wife's cost of insurance is not a part of the income calculation). From that $2,400, there is $2,150 left. In the state, the MMMNA is $2,739. What does that mean? Up to $2,139 can be diverted to the wife from what is remaining of her husband's income. The balance of $19 must be paid to the nursing home each month. From that income, the wife now must continue paying the electric, gas bill, and grocery bill; auto gasoline, insurance, and maintenance; house maintenance, insurance, and taxes (hopefully not a mortgage payment); her own health insurance supplement, doctor, and pharmacy bills; and her own personal everyday needs.

When the husband dies, she will lose her $600 and probably all or half of his pension. She will go from receiving $2,739 a month down to $1,200 or $1,800 a month.

Now, by changing a few numbers we can illustrate how harsh the MMMNA can be for individuals that are used to a slightly different lifestyle.

MMMNA Example No. 2—Drastic Lifestyle Alteration:

In this example, the community spouse still has her $600 Social Security check from working at a bank for a few years, but she became a teacher later in life and is now a retired teacher. So she has a small income, but she actually has a very large teacher's pension and gets $2,100 a month for her pension. Her husband is also a retired teacher (he was a principal) and has $4,000 a month for his teacher's pension.

Thus, the income in his name is $4,000. The income in the wife's name is now $2,700. He gets to keep $30 for the personal-needs allowance. His teacher pension provides his insurance, so there's no deduction for a Medicare supplement. In some states, $39 per month is all that is going to be diverted to the community spouse, the wife, because that brings her up to the $2,739 maximum.

What happens to the rest of his money? Now $3,961 must be paid to the nursing home, and the state pays only the difference—which truthfully won't be much, due to the fact that the state does not pay the private-pay rate but pays a much smaller daily rate in most cases.

Here we have a wife who was used to living on $6,700 a month between her husband and herself and now she's down to $2,739. That's quite a change!

These examples illustrate the application of nursing home Medicaid rules within one example state. Since those rules vary from state to state, is extremely important to get expert legal counsel with in the state in which an individual intends to become a nursing home resident.

Spend Down Traps and Opportunities

If a loved one has Alzheimer's and needs to qualify for Medicaid, but their assets are too high, that person cannot simply give away assets until reaching the maximum asset figure. Spending down must be done within Medicaid regulations.

You need to keep in mind that there is a **five-year look-back period** when it comes to assets and qualifying for Medicaid. That means if a loved one has Alzheimer's and needs to qualify for Medicaid, any gifts they made in the last five years can, and probably will, be scrutinized by the government. It is important to document everything.

Improper spending down should be a real fear. There's a chance more and more seniors will be dumped in the emergency room and will be disqualified from Medicaid, due to improper spending down. Not only will people who improperly spend down their assets be ineligible for Medicaid, but they won't be able to afford private care. Unfortunately, there's no long-term care facility that's going to take them. It is crucial that you speak with an attorney and make sure you fully understand how to properly spend down assets to qualify for Medicaid.

Individuals with more countable assets than allowed by Medicaid must "**pay down**" or "**spend down**" their assets before they can qualify for Medicaid benefits. If someone applies for Medicaid before "spending down" to the allowable countable asset level, some states will deny the application and others will place the applicant in a "spend-down" and require that all assets over the allowable amount be spent on care before eligibility is triggered. Although that might seem harmless, it is not!

This is an actual email that one of the authors received from a client:

I don't know if you can help me. My mom doesn't have a lot of assets. She owns a home and she has about $42,000 in other assets. She went into the hospital, but she wasn't there long enough before being transferred to a **skilled nursing facility**—nursing home rehab. Will she lose everything?

Typically, a person who is being transferred to a skilled nursing facility is either going to a nursing home for long-term care or for short-term care in a **skilled rehabilitation center**.

At that point, the nursing home will usually volunteer to work with the family to submit a Medicaid application for long-term care. If they provide the nursing home employee with the income and the asset information *and* she is then approved for a spend-down, the remaining $42,000 plus any sale proceeds from the home (in states where the home will not remain exempt) MUST be spent on care. Nursing home employees rarely have any training in nursing home Medicaid related asset protection law. They will complete a Medicaid application for the sole purpose of being properly paid for the care that they provide. Once a Medicaid application is filed by a nursing home, it would need to be withdrawn prior to approval for the client to take advantage of any legally authorized and legitimate asset protection strategies.

There are a lot of "what ifs" that go unanswered when the family allows a nursing home to file the Medicaid application.

- Could something have been done to start the penalty or cure it so she didn't end up destitute and with Medicaid refusing to pay until the penalty is over? Yes.
- Could she have used some of the $42,000 to hire a lawyer to do her estate plan and review her five years of records? Yes.
- Could she have used some of the $42,000 to prepay her funeral expenses? Yes.
- Could she have paid off her credit card debt and her real estate taxes? Yes.
- Can she do these things now, after she has applied and been put in a spend-down? No. All of the $42,000 must be paid to the nursing home and all the proceeds from the sale of the home as well.

Almost all of these "what ifs" could be legitimately paid before filing a Medicaid application.

There are also hidden dangers that can trap a senior and cause a penalty period of ineligibility for nursing home Medicaid coverage. If she made any gifts, then she could lose Medicaid coverage. After an application is denied and a penalty period imposed, it will be too late to cure those penalty creating gifts,

Your state Medicaid department has a surprising broad view of what constitutes an unallowable gift. One of the author's clients once said,

"They just are not allowing families to be families anymore!" Other clients have said, "How are they, the state, going to know whether I gave my money away?" The answer to that question is this: The burden is not on the state to discover whether or not you gave money away; rather the burden is on the Medicaid applicant to prove that every single financial transaction during the 16 months prior to the Medicaid application was legally permissible by the state Medicaid rules. You are assumed to know all of the law and to have abided by the law and if you failed to fulfill the law then you will be denied nursing home Medicaid coverage. This is not a do-it- yourself project!

Gifts can be classified as "**non-allowable transfers**" if made during the five years preceding a Medicaid nursing home application. The transfers would be lumped-together as a total and a penalty assessed—and that penalty will not start to run until the senior-Medicaid-applicant is "otherwise eligible," which means not until he or she has completed her spend-down. Then the penalty period will begin, and he or she won't get benefits until it ends. In many states, 100 percent of what the state characterizes as a gift must be repaid by the recipients to cure a penalty which denies nursing home Medicaid coverage.

Document the Reason for Gifts to Family Members

The Medicaid Department rules in most states create a **rebuttable presumption** that all gifts given by seniors to their family members were done for the sole purpose of impoverishing themselves so as to be able to qualify for nursing home Medicaid. You can rebut that presumption with evidence. The evidence needs to be done at the time of the gift. You can imagine how difficult it is once a person has Alzheimer's disease or other dementia to be able to prove the reason that money was transferred between family members.

It is a good idea to have a lawyer help you create a contemporaneous written statement about any transfers of money as a gift. Creating a written statement provides some evidence that will help rebut the presumption that money was given away to qualify for Medicaid. The document should say, for example, "Here are the facts and circumstances that surround my gift of $20,000 to my beloved daughter Marilyn. Marilyn needed $20,000 for emergency surgery due to an injury incurred in a car accident." (Attach a copy of the hospital bills.)

79

The IRS Gift Tax Exemption Is Irrelevant to the State Medicaid Department

Individuals can give away up to $15,000 (in 2018) per recipient without filing a gift tax return with the Internal Revenue Service.

One of the most common myths of gifting is that the *recipient* of the gift pays taxes. It is counterintuitive to think that the person *making* a gift may be responsible for gift taxes on the amount gifted—but that's how it works! You can give away money, and if you don't go beyond the lifetime limit, you are likely to have no *gift tax* issues. However, you will certainly have *Medicaid* problems if you need nursing home care within five years of the date of the gift. Even though the IRS exempted you from filing a gift tax return, when and if you need to file for a Medicaid application, the state will include all of those gifts within their computation for the determination of the penalty period of ineligibility for nursing Home Medicaid benefits. As stated above, you are responsible for providing sufficient evidence that there was some valid reason that motivated you to make a gift.

Nursing Home Medicaid Myths and Big Money Mistakes

The purpose of this book is to give you general information that you can use to help a loved one affected by Alzheimer's disease and their family. We will list a number of beliefs and mistakes that we have seen people make that can be extremely costly. After reading this general information we strongly encourage you to reach out to a highly trained and experienced elder law attorney in your state for specific guidance.

Revocable Living Trusts/Living Trusts and Irrevocable Asset Protection Trusts

Many people have done estate planning in which they have used a **revocable living trust** which is also known as a living trust. The authors have had innumerable people tell them that they believe that their living trust provides asset protection that will keep their money from being used for long-term care services. The statement usually goes something like this, "I'm not worried about losing my money to the nursing home because I have it all in a trust." Almost 100 percent of the time the person making that statement or the family member making that statement about their parent mistakenly believes that a living trust creates a financial fortress around its assets. Nothing could be further from the truth!

A revocable living trust is a wonderful foundational trust. Its use is to organize assets; name successor trustees; name future beneficiaries; and to avoid probate after the death of the trust maker. The law of every state treats a revocable living trust as the legal equivalent of an individual's wallet or purse. Since the individual can put money in and take money out, then any asset is available to be spent on that individual's long-term care costs. As discussed earlier in this chapter, any asset that is available for Medicaid applicant is treated as a countable asset. All countable assets have a limit. Prior to qualifying for Medicaid assistance for long-term care services the burden of proof is on the applicant to show that they do not have any available assets in excess of the limit.

There are other types of trusts which are legally recognized as creating a fortress around assets and money. Those trusts are generally referred to as **Irrevocable Asset Protection Trusts**.

There are a wide variety of Irrevocable Asset Protection Trusts. The authors provide their clients with both revocable living trust and irrevocable asset protection trusts. These trusts need to be properly drafted to meet both state and federal guidelines. An improperly drafted trust will not be upheld in a court of law. You must have a properly drafted trust for it to be able to transform available/countable assets into *legally unavailable assets.*

There are a number of important ingredients that must go into a recipe to create a satisfactory final product when using an asset protection trust. Capable legal practitioners who focus in this particular niche know the right ingredients.

Please be advised that this tool is not right for everyone. The assets transferred to the trust cannot be returned to the person who put the funds in the trust. Nonetheless, the Trustmaker's do retain certain powers such as to be able to change trustees and beneficiaries. This is one of the most frequently used tools for Medicaid related asset protection. Since it must it be in existence for five years prior to a Medicaid application, an appropriate situation would be one in which there are sufficient available funds to pay through five years before applying for Medicaid benefits.

This is what we refer to as Five Year Planning. One is basically making an allocation between a portion of the estate that will be spent and a portion of the estate that will be protected.

Prenuptial Agreements and Nursing Home Medicaid

It is common for seniors to get married to other seniors. In many of those situations, the seniors are the widowed survivors of a prior marriage. Those seniors frequently have children from those prior marriages. The seniors wish to be married for many reasons, including companionship.

Nonetheless, they often seek to keep their finances separate so as to preserve the inheritance rights of their own children.

Many seniors seek to reassure their own children that they will not lose their inheritance by entering into an agreement in which the husband and wife promise each other that they will not look to the other for long-term care costs. In the majority of the cases that the authors have experienced those agreements are informal. In some cases, they have been reduced to writing by the couple. Prenuptial agreements may have been drafted by attorneys. Regardless of the manner in which those promises have been undertaken, when it comes to the liability pay for health-care expenses those agreements are ineffective.

Since the Middle Ages, it has been understood in English common law that husbands and wives have a duty to pay for the necessary expenses incurred for each other. Those necessary expenses have always included the cost of health care. In these modern times, the former common law has become written law in every state. Health-care providers and their lobbyists have secured written laws which expressly create a duty for husbands and wives to pay for each other's health care. In other words, even though the husband and wife have promised each other not to expect their spouse to pay for care, the health-care provider is not a party to that contract. The health-care provider can demand payment from a spouse and a court will uphold that demand.

Now let's look at this in the context of nursing home care. Nursing home care is a type of health- care. When one of the spouses needs nursing home care, the assets of both of the spouses are deemed to be available assets/countable assets. This has come as a big surprise to many people who have sought the asset protection counsel of the authors.

This is another situation in which it is sometimes wise to use an asset protection trust in which each spouse allocates a portion of their own money which they hope to keep protected for their children. Each spouse has a separate asset protection trust and they can appoint one or more of their honest and reliable children to serve as trustees. If those trusts are allowed to age over 60 months, then those assets become legally unavailable and are off the radar screen for Medicaid purposes.

Medicaid Compliant Annuities Compared to Other Annuities

Normal annuities purchase from the usual sources such as insurance company salespeople and other financial advisors are considered available/countable assets. As you know, a Medicaid applicant has a countable asset limit. Only one type of annuity is structured in a way that allows the Medicaid applicant to have their cake and eat it too. That annuity is not an annuity that you would normally purchase through the usual sources. It is not annuity that you would purchase as a normal investment oriented annuity decision. This annuity type was designed to fit federal law and should only be used in the context when one is seeing long-term nursing home care in the headlights. This tool was erected in 1988 by Senator Ted Kennedy, deceased.

A **Medicaid Compliant Annuity (MCA)** is an asset preservation and income enhancement strategy that was originally put into the federal law to permit single individuals and married couples to have a better outcome. This particular strategy has been upheld in numerous federal appellate court cases. The facts and circumstances of the situation must be evaluated by experienced practitioners who understand both the law and the math that underlie this strategy.

The bottom line is that money that would have had to have been consumed as an available asset will be transformed into an allowable income stream. Rules vary depending on the state of your residence. The proper structuring of this strategy results in a nursing home applicant receiving Medicaid benefits and the healthier spouse receiving a higher monthly income.

Federal law, the Deficit Reduction Act of 2005, required that for an annuity to be Medicaid compliant, it must be an unusual type of annuity. It must have all of the following features:

1. be irrevocable
2. be nonassignable
3. be actuarially sound in that it pay out its interest and principal over the life expectancy of the annuitant
4. in the event that the primary beneficiary dies, most states require that they be the contingent beneficiary of the annuity

Medicaid compliant annuities can be funded with almost any liquid asset. That would include tax-deferred accounts such as an IRA.

Medicaid compliant annuities can be used in the single person Medicaid situation and the married couple Medicaid benefit fact pattern. A skilled elder law attorney can pair the purchase of a Medicaid compliant annuity with the gifting of appropriate assets and still achieve nursing Home Medicaid benefit approval. This is no easy task and one in which it is well worth hiring a professional elder law attorney to assist you.

Caretaker Child Living with Parent(s)

Nursing Home Medicaid rules are not like hand grenades and horseshoes. Getting close does not count for anything. You have to follow the rules exactly. Here's an example of the very valuable exception to the harsh rules that restrict a senior from gifting their home to their children.

Federal law provides an incentive for an adult child of the senior to move into the home of the senior who needs long-term care. After moving in, the child must provide substantial care for the senior who would otherwise need to be in a nursing home facility. The quality of the care provided by the child must be sufficient so that the senior does not need to move to the nursing home for a minimum of two years. In other words the caretaker child must provide two full years of in-home care to their parent or parents. That parent must be in need of long-term care services equivalent to a nursing home. Evidence must be provided from a physician indicating that the parent had such a condition. The child must provide actual proof that they lived in the home.

That proof would include such things as change of address; change of place of voting; and other factors that would support the fact that the child moved into the home.

If sufficient evidence has been provided to support the caretaker child exception; then the state Medicaid department will allow the senior to transfer their home to their adult child. There is no limitation on the value of the home. There is no comparison between the fair market value of the home and the fair market value of the actual services that were rendered to the senior. This is a strange and wonderful incentive to provide compensation to an honest and reliable child who is willing to work hard to keep their parent at home for a minimum of two years.

This caretaker child exception is only available when and if a natural born child or adopted child provides the caregiving services for the parent. This exception is not available if a stepchild or a grandchild or any other relative provides the same services.

Medicare, Medicare Supplemental Insurance, Medigap Insurance, Medicare Advantage

Many people believe that Medicare will pay for long-term care services. That is a myth. Many people believe that **Medicare Supplemental Insurance** and/or **Medigap Insurance** will pay for long-term care services. The reason that they believe this is that they say, "I was told that my Medicare supplemental insurance would pay for whatever Medicare did not pay for." This error is understandable. People have been told to buy a Medicare supplemental insurance plan for the purpose of paying the Medicare deductible. Medicare is covered in full in Chapter 5. Medicare is designed to pay for hospital, doctor, and rehab care. The federal government pays a national average of 65 percent of the medical costs incurred by a Medicare recipient for a medical procedure for which there is a Medicare Reimbursement Code. A Medicare supplemental insurance plan is designed to pay the average 35 percent shortfall, after Medicare has paid its share. In other words, Medicare is the first payer and then, a Medicare supplemental insurance plan is the second payer. It is important to note, that if Medicare does not pay anything then the Medicare supplemental insurance plan also pays nothing.

Family Member Caregiver Contracts

Unfortunately, the state Medicaid department is very unforgiving. It is very common and normal for family members to be providing care and help to lengthen the amount of time that a loved one affected by Alzheimer's can continue to stay home. As the affected persons needs grow, many times, an honest and reliable child is transporting them to various locations such as doctor appointments; purchasing drugs and groceries; paying numerous other bills out of pocket; and running many other errands. These situations often start out innocently with things like picking up groceries for Mom and Dad, driving them to their appointments, and maybe giving them $100 here and there. This can quickly transition into the caregiver children preparing meals, cleaning, doing the laundry, and stopping by at least once a day to check on them. At some point, a child may even decide to quit his or her job because taking care of Mom or Dad has become a full–time job.

It is extremely unlikely that these family members are keeping track of their receipts and/or mileage.

And what are Mom and Dad doing? They are writing checks to the caregiver child for gas, for food, and for time spent cleaning and doing laundry. The adult child is taking care of Mom and Dad and frequently the money becomes co-mingled. The child is buying her groceries and their groceries together. The parents are paying some and the adult child is paying some.

In some cases, a child moves in with the parents to provide better care for them. Maybe the child is also the power of attorney for property, or at least, the power of attorney for health care.

Maybe the parents add the child to their bank accounts so the child can pay bills for them, including reimbursements to the child.

The scenario often is that a dutiful daughter, who is also the power of attorney, is taking care of the parents' accounts and is writing herself checks to cover her expenses, and also to cover the fact that she has left gainful employment to take care of her parents. Some states' laws consider what she is doing to be elder abuse! She may certainly be violating the power of attorney statute. The time comes that the parents require a higher level of care than she can provide, and one or both of the parents go to a nursing home and apply for Medicaid. All those checks written by the daughter will now be scrutinized by the state. The caregiver/daughter may be accused of elder abuse, and the parents may have a penalty period of ineligibility for nursing home Medicaid benefits.

If there was no contract in place between the parents and the daughter outlining the care to be provided and the compensation to be paid, the state will consider the transfers as non-allowable.

Therefore, you need to create a powerful caretaker contract to avoid these unwanted consequences.

Powerful Caretaker Child Contract

The first step you should do is to hire a geriatric care manager or other professional to create a personalized care plan for the individual with Alzheimer's disease. Then have your attorney draft a caregiver contract that is tied to the care that the care manager says needs to be done. The care manager can highlight what can be done by a non-licensed individual.

This approach provides a very personal plan rather than relying on a generic contract. As always, we suggest that you keep written records of all spending.

You may need your attorney to modify the statutory power of attorney to specifically state that the child, as the agent under the power of attorney, has authority to hire themselves on behalf of the parents, the principals, as a caregiver. A lot more goes into drafting a good caregiver contract than one might think. You have to remember that all of these financial decisions and contracts will be reviewed by the attorneys work for the state Medicaid department. It is their job to find legitimate reasons to deny or delay the claim that is being submitted on behalf of the person affected by Alzheimer's disease. It's sad; but it's true. Take all necessary measures to assure the financial transactions between parent and child will pass muster with the state.

After a properly drafted caregiver agreement has been created, consult with an accountant to determine how and if employment taxes must be handled. In many cases family members who serve as caregivers do not owe self-employment tax on any payments they receive for caring for a family member, unless the family caregiver is in the business of providing care to others. For example, if a daughter is a nurse and happens to be taking care of her dad after is diagnosed with dementia, then in that case, the daughter may have to pay self-employment tax.

When a Medicaid application is submitted, the state will treat all monies transferred to the child as gifts. It is presumed under the law that family members are providing help for a senior purely for love and affection. It is important to remember that gifts are the basis of creating penalty periods of eligibility for Medicaid care for the senior.

To avoid the situation, and to comply with state law, a written caregiver contract must be created that very specifically list the duties and the compensation.

We hope that this chapter has provided you with more hope. There is more than ample reason for the family of a person affected by Alzheimer's disease to seek the counsel of experienced professionals in their state. Those professionals which include care managers, elder law attorneys, and in support groups can help you find the best care options and asset/income strategies.

Documents Needed for a Nursing Home Medicaid Application

GENERAL INFORMATION

For both applicant and spouse:

- ❑ ID card and/or driver's license/Social Security card (if available)
- ❑ Medical cards—Medicare, Supplemental Medical Insurance, Prescription Drug Card (front and back)
- ❑ Birth certificate (may be obtained from the county of birth)
- ❑ Marriage license (if spouse is living)
- ❑ Death Certificate (if spouse is deceased)
- ❑ Divorce Decree (if divorced)
- ❑ Power of Attorney for property (not health care)

INCOME/EXPENSE INFO

For both applicant and spouse:

- ❑ Annual Social Security award letter for this year
- ❑ Pension income information (most recent info) for this year which shows GROSS and NET amount of payment (*NOT* a 1099)
- ❑ Supplemental Medical Insurance Invoice
- ❑ Medicare Part D Invoice
- ❑ Long-term care Insurance Contract and Premium Invoice
- ❑ Any other monthly income

GENERAL ASSETS

For both applicant and spouse:

- ❑ Deed(s) to residence and any other property
- ❑ Homeowners Insurance Policy
- ❑ If house/property has been sold in the past 60 months—settlement statement from closing
- ❑ Realtor's Comparative Market Analysis / Appraisal
- ❑ Most recent property tax bill
- ❑ Title to car
- ❑ Auto Insurance Policy
- ❑ Funeral plan
- ❑ Burial deed
- ❑ Life insurance—cash and face value
- ❑ List of contents in safe deposit box

TAX RETURNS

For the last five years:

- ❏ Federal and state income tax returns with schedules and attachments

- ❏ Copies of all 1099s and W2 forms, even if no return was filed

ACCOUNT STATEMENTS

For applicant (and spouse if applicable) For the last five years:

- ❏ All account statements during the Review Period of 60 months, **whether open or closed**.

- ❏ (Statements may be annual, quarterly, or monthly, depending upon the account.)

- ❏ Copies of cancelled checks, deposit slips with copies of the checks that were the source of the deposit, and supporting documentation for withdrawals (where deposited or receipts for purchases), must be included with the statements for all transactions of $1,000 and over.

- ❏ Checking accounts

- ❏ Savings accounts

- ❏ CDs (Transaction History)

- ❏ Stock/Bonds

- ❏ IRAs

- ❏ Annuities

- ❏ Money Market

- ❏ Investment Accounts

Note: After filing, the Department of Human Services caseworker may request additional documentation.

CHAPTER 7

AVOIDING THE HIDDEN TRAPS OF NURSING HOME CONTRACTS

The purpose of this chapter is to give you general information that you can use to help a loved one affected by Alzheimer's disease and their family. Below, you will find information on nursing homes and nursing home contracts, including a number of beliefs and mistakes that we have seen people make that can be extremely costly. After reading this general information we strongly encourage you to reach out to a highly trained and experienced elder law attorney in your state for specific guidance.

To-Do Checklist

❑ Accept that nursing home care is often unavoidable

❑ Understand what to look for in a nursing home for your loved one

❑ Learn what hidden dangers lurk in nursing home contracts and how to circumvent them

❑ Know what rights your loved one retains in a nursing home

Most of the nursing homes in the United States are owned by regional and/or national multiple-site corporations. Large corporations can afford to employ excellent lawyers who have the benefit of focusing exclusively on the long-term-care facility niche. Those lawyers know the law, the regulations, and the cases. The nursing home chains are keenly aware of what commonly causes them to lose money.

You can be assured that nursing homes have demanded that their legal counsel draft nursing home contracts to put potential residents at a disadvantage. When your family lawyer reviews a nursing home contract for you, they are at a distinct disadvantage. A highly knowledgeable opponent drafted the contract to make sure that the nursing home was not going to lose money. We advise you have an elder law attorney who is familiar with these contracts at your side.

Nursing Home Care Is Often Unavoidable

Recent studies reveal that nearly 70 percent of those 65 and older will eventually need some sort of long-term care assistance. Fortunately; most people will not require full-time nursing home services. When a family reaches the point when it becomes necessary for an affected loved one to enter a nursing home, it is one of the most difficult decisions one ever has to make. When Alzheimer's disease has progressed to the point where the affected loved one can no longer live alone, or when the primary caregiver can no longer provide the level or expertise of care that is necessary, a move to a nursing home is the next stop on the Alzheimer's care journey.

There are companies that specialize in connecting prospective nursing facility residents with facilities. One nationwide organization is called A Place for Mom (www.aplaceformom.com). This type of organization makes its money by being paid a commission by the long-term-care facility. Because the organization is paid on commission, it is important to understand that they may not have listing contracts with all facilities; therefore, you may not be shown the entire panorama of options. This statement is not meant to be critical, but rather to express the possible limitations of such services.

The Centers for Medicare and Medicaid Services rate nursing homes and publish the results. The system is called the Nursing Home Compare. It includes ratings of nursing homes based on quality measurements, staffing ratios, and health inspections. The website is www.medicare.gov/NursingHomeCompare.

Once you have found a few facilities that look like good options, you should visit each one several times, preferably at different times in the day and at least once during a meal.

It is important to find a nursing home with an Alzheimer's special-care unit. Alzheimer's sufferers have unique needs and will have a much better nursing home experience if the nursing home staff is capable of dealing with their needs. Staff in special-care units should take specialized training courses in order to be able to encourage the residents' independence and help them realize the maximum potential of their mental and physical abilities as their dementia progresses.

Nursing Homes with Special Alzheimer's Units

You should look for the following qualities from a nursing home with a special unit before agreeing to pay the higher rate:

- Does the facility confirm all incoming residents' Alzheimer's diagnosis?

- Is the staff aware of the progressive nature of Alzheimer's disease, and how do they address the expected changes in the mental and physical abilities of the residents?

- Are all of the employees in the special unit (the housekeepers, maintenance workers, etc.) given some training regarding Alzheimer's?

- Are the buildings and grounds designed for people suffering from Alzheimer's disease?

- Are the resident activities appropriate for people with Alzheimer's?

It is important to keep in mind that this type of care is expensive. Fees average around $55,000 a year nationwide and can be as expensive as $100,000 or more. Most insurance plans do not cover this type of long-term care and neither does Medicare.

Fortunately, Medicaid is available for qualified individuals. Medicaid is a federally funded, state- administered medical assistance program that is explained in detail in Chapter 6.

Nursing home contracts are supposed to include language informing the people signing the contract that they should consult with a lawyer. However, this language is usually going to be in small print and is usually buried in the contract. You should definitely have your elder law lawyer review the contract with you. Most non-lawyers may not know, or may be afraid, to strike through parts of a contract that they don't agree with.

Even though nursing home contracts should be reviewed by legal counsel, the majority of nursing home contracts are not brought to the attention of a lawyer until a problem has arisen after admission and the contract has been signed. In the author's experience, few people engage an attorney before signing a nursing home contract.

Potential Pitfalls in Nursing Home Contracts: Do Not Sign as a Responsible Party

There can be several potential traps in nursing home contract language. The best thing to do is to draw a line through the offending language. For example, many nursing home contracts will "request" that someone else sign along with the potential resident. When author Rick Law was in law school, his business law professor stated emphatically, "A cosigner is a fool with a pen in his hand." Those excellent lawyers who have written the nursing home contracts have crafted many legal ways to attempt to turn family members into cosigners who are referred to as a "**responsible party**." When a non-lawyer (layperson) who is either an **agent** under a **health-care power of attorney**, caregiver under a **personal-care agreement**, or an honest and reliable child carrying the burden of decision-making sees the words "responsible party," they do not think that to be synonymous with "cosigner."

The use of the words "responsible party" in this case leads to many people being deceived into becoming a cosigner for the affected loved one. Assuming the role of "responsible party" means that the person is assuming liability for any debts created by the resident.

Arbitration Clauses: Proceed with Caution

Always remember that the lawyers working for the nursing homes and creating those nursing home contracts are serving the needs of the nursing home first and foremost. They are paid to protect the nursing home. One of the ways they are protecting nursing homes is by inserting arbitration clauses in the resident contracts. As you or your lawyer review any contract, you should be on alert for the presence of such clauses. Nursing homes are raising arbitration clauses as a defense, even in cases of wrongful death actions and personal injury suits.

Residents' Rights

Just because your loved one is in a nursing home does not mean they give up all of their rights. There is a federal law, the Federal Nursing Home Reform Act, which lays out the rights of nursing home residents. This law states that a nursing home facility is required by law to protect and promote the rights of each resident. Here is a list of some (but not all) of those rights that your loved ones are still entitled to:

1. The right to make financial and medical decisions—to the extent the resident has the capacity to do so.

2. The right to be free of interference, coercion, discrimination, and reprisal from the facility in exercising their rights.

3. If your loved one is incapacitated due to his or her Alzheimer's, their rights may be exercised by the person appointed under state law to act on the resident's behalf.

4. The facility must inform the resident (both orally and in writing in a language that the resident understands) of the resident's rights and all rules and regulations governing resident conduct and responsibilities during the stay in the facility.

5. The right to access all records pertaining to the resident, including current clinical records within 24 hours of making a request to see the records (excluding weekends and holidays).

6. The resident has the right to be fully informed in language that the resident can understand of their total health status.

7. The resident has the right to refuse treatment, to refuse to participate in experimental research, and to create an **advance directive**.

8. The facility must inform residents that are entitled to Medicaid benefits which items and services are included in the nursing facility services charges and which items and services would cause extra charges.

This must be done in writing.

Loved ones in nursing homes are entitled to manage their personal finances and choose their health-care providers. They should not sign a contract that requires them to deposit personal funds with the facility.

The nursing home must keep your loved one informed of any plan of care and any changes in that plan and must allow them to be an active participant in their own health-care plan. This includes allowing them to refuse treatment. Just because people are residents of a nursing home doesn't mean they lose their rights.

Nursing homes must assess a resident's needs every 12 months and create a health-care plan appropriate to the needs of the particular resident. Your loved one is entitled to have a lawyer present with them (or the resident's representative if the resident no longer has capacity to make health-care decisions) to ensure that the resident's best interests are served by the health-care plan.

Check the applicable specific services being provided for the care recipient:

❑ Help with dressing

❑ Training for substitute/additional caregiver

❑ Help with bathing

❑ Supervision to prevent care recipient from harming himself

❑ Help with ambulating

❑ Supervision to prevent care recipient from harming others

❑ Help with toileting

❑ Help with incontinence

❑ Providing a protective environment for cognitive impairment

❑ Providing restraint or direction if care recipient is uncooperative

❑ Medication reminders

❑ Physical therapy

❑ Help with feeding

❑ Administration of medications

❑ Providing meals

❑ Placement of catheters

❑ Homemaker services

❑ Changing sterile dressings

❑ Supervision to prevent wandering

❑ Transportation or transportation assistance

CHAPTER 8

WARTIME VETERANS BENEFITS FOR LONG-TERM CARE: WORLD WAR II– THE MIDEAST CONFLICTS

The authors wish to thank Victoria L. Collier, www.elderlawgeorgia.com, Certified Elder Law Attorney, Fellow of the National Academy of Elder Law Attorneys, Co–Founder of Veterans Advocates Group of America, Author of *47 Secret Veterans' Benefits for Seniors: Benefits You Earned but Don't Know About,* national speaker and trainer on Veterans Pension benefits, and a wartime veteran of the United States Air Force.

Attorney Collier took time from her very busy schedule to review the initial draft of this book and provide substantial refinement for the benefit of our readers who may be veterans themselves and/or members of the family of our beloved and courageous wartime veterans.

Jack and Nell are an example of a couple who have sacrificed to serve our country during a time of war. There are specific VA benefits which can be of assistance to both the veteran and the veterans' surviving spouse.

Real-Life Story: Jack and Nell

More than a decade ago, author Rick Law received a call from Jack and Nell's son. Jack (deceased) had been a friend of the family and mentor to Rick since Rick was a teenager.

Nell was diagnosed with Parkinson's disease, and needed full-time skilled nursing care. The son and his wife were caring for Nell in their own home. The son knew that Jack had been an air-sea rescue pilot during World War II, and wanted to know if there were any veterans' benefits that could help pay for his mother's care in a care facility.

We explained that there is an important VA benefit available to wartime veterans (and their widows) who may be facing substantial medical and long-term care expenses. These benefits may also help a veteran who is confined to home or needs an assisted living facility or nursing home to provide care.

The son told us that his dad had not been wounded during his time of service and asked if that made his mom ineligible for long-term care benefits. We assured him that even though there were many rules and restrictions, this particular benefit was based on military service during a wartime period. A veteran did not need to have been injured during the actual time of service. The veteran also did not have to have been retired from the military.

The benefit is commonly referred to as Aid & Attendance. The VA does not refer to it by that name, however, which can lead to confusion when trying to access long-term care benefits for a wartime veteran or surviving spouse. The formal name of the benefit is the Improved Pension. **This benefit is limited specifically to veterans who have served during designated wartime periods, and their surviving spouse.**

We were able to share with the family the good news that there were some funds available due to Jack's qualification as a wartime veteran. We then worked with them to put their estate planning documentation in order and to represent them in filing an appropriate VA claim for long-term care benefits to help pay for Nell's expenses at an assisted living facility.

While the benefit was not sufficient to pay all of Nell's cost of care, it was a valuable addition to the resources available.

Veterans' Benefits in a Nutshell

The U.S. federal Veterans Administration provides a multitude of different services and veterans' benefits, including the most well-known health-care services and compensation for service connected disabilities (injured while in the military). This chapter will; however, focus exclusively on the lesser known benefit, the **Improved Pension** also known as, Special Monthly Pension, Aid and Attendance, or Non-Service Connected Pension.

Non-Service-Connected Pension

Veteran

- Must be permanently and totally disabled, or 65 years of age or older. Disability does not have to be related to military duty
- Pension is needs-based—must meet income and net worth requirements; or
- If the veteran has too much income or too many assets, he/she will not qualify for the pension
- A higher pension is awarded if the veteran is housebound
- An even higher pension if the veteran is in need of regular aid and attendance

Spouse/Dependent

- Eligible for Death Pension
- A higher pension is awarded if the spouse/dependent is housebound
- An even higher pension if the spouse/dependent is in need of regular aid and attendance

Did you serve during one of the VA Defined War Periods?

- World War II: December 7, 1941–December 31, 1946
- Korean Conflict: June 27, 1950–January 31, 1955
- Vietnam Era: August 5, 1964–May 7, 1975. Veterans who served February 28, 1961–August 5, 1964 must have served "in country" (Vietnam).

- Persian Gulf War: August 2, 1990–date to be prescribed by Presidential Proclamation or law. Must have served active duty for two years.

Who is eligible for the non-service-connected pension?

- Honorably discharged veterans, surviving spouses, or dependent children of any military, naval, or air service. Also includes certain other special groups such as:
  - Women's Army Auxiliary Corps (WAAC)
  - Merchant Marines from WWII
  - U.S. civilians of the American Field Service
  - Plus 30 more! (See list later in this guide.)
- Served in active duty 90 days, one of which was during a period of war
- *At least 65 years old OR Permanently and Totally Disabled*

"Permanently and Totally Disabled" is defined as:

- Medical necessity of long-term care for the rest of his/her life; or
- Receiving Social Security disability benefits; or
- Unemployable as a result of disability reasonably certain to continue throughout the life of the person.

The veteran's current disability does not need to have any connection to the veteran's actual time in the armed forces. (Non-service-connected disability can be Alzheimer's, Parkinson's, etc.)

Other requirements: This is a needs-based program with income and asset tests.

Income limitation

- Gross income MINUS certain expenses:
  - Unreimbursed medical expenses of veteran and his/her household
  - Certain educational expenses
- After reducing gross income by the above expenses, net income must be so low that the veteran's assets and income are insufficient to pay for their own medical needs.

Net worth limitation

In addition to your house, car, life insurance, burial policies, and annuities in payout status, you can generally have between $50,000 and $80,000 in assets, including CDs, stocks, bonds, and retirement accounts.

A More Complete Explanation

The improved pension is a monthly, tax free income benefit for veterans or their surviving spouses who have a low income. The veteran must be 65 years of age or older to receive the pension, but there is no minimum age for surviving spouses. Moreover, neither the veteran nor the surviving spouse need be disabled.

In addition to the pension, the veteran or widow may receive an increased benefit called a special monthly pension if it can be shown that they are either housebound or in need of aid and attendance because they are permanently and totally disabled. The disability does *not* have to be related to military service.

Veterans are considered to have a permanent and total disability if they are:

- patients in a nursing home for long-term care because of disability;
- receiving Social Security Disability benefits;
- unemployable as a result of a disability that is reasonably certain to continue throughout their life; or
- suffering from any disease or disorder determined by the Secretary of the Department of Veterans Affairs to be a permanent or total disability.

In 2018 the maximum disability pension rate for a veteran with no dependents was $13,166 annually, which worked out to $1,097 per month. The rate for a veteran with one dependent, or for two veterans married to each other, was $17,241 annually, or $1,436 per month.

The amount of the special monthly pension increases if the veteran with permanent disabilities is also "**housebound**." People are considered housebound if they have a permanent and total disability and either have additional disability estimated at 60 percent or more, or are substantially confined to their residence or the immediate premises due to a disability that is reasonably certain to remain throughout their lifetime.

In 2018 the maximum pension for a housebound veteran with no dependents was $16,089 annually, or $1,340 per month. If the housebound veteran had one dependent, the maximum pension was $20,166 annually, or $1,680 per month. If a surviving spouse was housebound, the maximum pension was $10,792 annually, or $899 per month.

If the veteran is in need of regular aid and attendance, the special monthly pension was increased further to a maximum of $21,962 annually, or $1,830 per month (using 2018 figures) if the veteran had no dependents. With one dependent, the maximum pension in 2018 was $26,036 annually, or $2,169 per month. If the surviving spouse is housebound, the maximum pension was $14,113 annually, or $1,176 per month. To be in need of regular aid and attendance, the veteran or spouse must have a permanent or total disability and be (1) a patient in a nursing home; (2) blind, or nearly blind; or (3) needing the regular aid and attendance of another person to perform basic activities of daily living, such as dressing, bathing, eating, and attending to the wants of nature.

Income/Net Worth Requirements

In order to be eligible to receive any of the above non-service-connected pensions, the veteran must meet income and net worth requirements.

First, the annual maximum pension amount is decreased, dollar for dollar, by the veteran's countable income. Income that is "countable" is generally all of the veteran's gross income (prior to any deductions), including that of a spouse or any dependents, *minus* unreimbursed medical expenses.

Unreimbursed medical expenses include doctor fees, dentist fees, Medicare premiums and copayments, supplemental health insurance and long-term care insurance premiums, transportation to physician offices, and the costs of in-home aides, assisted living facilities or nursing homes.

In addition to low income, the veteran must also have limited net worth. The VA has not specifically defined "limited net worth" with a dollar amount; however, a general guide is that the veteran have a net worth less than $50,000.

Example:

If a single veteran has $20,000 in annual gross income and $10,000 in unreimbursed medical expenses, the countable income is $10,000. The $10,000 in countable income is deducted from the maximum annual pension rate of $13,166 for an annual benefit of $3,166, or a monthly benefit of $263.

As another example, suppose the veteran is in a nursing home (and so qualifies for the additional special monthly pension for aid and attendance) and has an income of $50,000. If the unreimbursed medical expenses for the nursing home are $5,000 per month or $60,000 annually, the veteran's countable income is negative $10,000. Any negative income is counted as an income of $0, and the veteran will be eligible for the maximum annual special monthly pension for Aid & Attendance of $21,962 for a veteran without dependents or $26,036 for a veteran with a dependent spouse or disabled child.

Death Pension

The VA pays a death pension to low income surviving spouses and unmarried dependent children of deceased wartime veterans. In order to be eligible, a spouse must not have remarried and a dependent must be under age 18, or under age 23 if attending a VA- approved school. Dependents who are permanently incapable of self-support because of disability before age 18 are also eligible for the death pension. The death pension may also include the special monthly payments for housebound and aid and attendance.

Proposed Obstacles to Obtaining Benefits

In January 2015 the Department of Veterans Affairs proposed substantial changes to the Improved Pension laws. The VA seeks to create legal barriers to what they perceived to be fraud. A number of legal and financial strategies were employed to intentionally reduce a veteran applicant's net worth and/or income so as to enable that veteran to qualify for their pension (often with aid & attendance). To eliminate or minimize the opportunity for veterans to legally impoverish themselves to qualify; the VA has proposed a number of very restrictive laws.

Some of the proposed changes will be positive changes for veterans and veterans' advocates. For example, having a bright-line dollar value of assessing net worth will provide clarity and certainty to eligibility issues. The bright-line figure is synonymous with the Federal Medicaid spousal impoverishment limit, which is $123,600. Any veteran having less than that amount would be eligible, if all other qualifications (military requirements, disability, and income) were met. It has been proposed that the asset limit would be indexed for inflation using the same inflation factor used by the Social Security Administration. Currently, and inconsistently, the VA uses the veteran's life expectancy as part of the determining factors in deciding the appropriate amount of assets. In other words, if a veteran was 85, they were assumed to have a shorter life span than a 70-year-old veteran. Assuming they each held the same value of assets, the 85-year-old may be denied benefits on the basis of having a sufficient amount to last their lifetime; whereas, the 70 year may be approved for benefits on the basis they would run out of assets during their lifetime.

The primary residence, and a reasonable lot area it sits on, has historically been an exempt asset from the net worth calculation. The lot area could be a quarter of an acre or well over 200 acres and it would remain exempt as long as the other properties in the vicinity are of the same approximate size. The VA has proposed that the primary residence on a parcel of land would only be exempt up to 2 acres. If and when the residence was sold, the money received would be considered countable toward the VA asset limit, unless the veteran or spouse reinvested the proceeds into the purchase of another residence within the same calendar year. This would negatively affect anyone who sold a home during the fourth quarter of the year.

Other proposed changes will negatively affect veterans, and affect different classes of applicants differently (i.e. single veteran vs. married veteran vs. widow).

Currently (as of early 2018), the VA does not have any written laws which forbid a veteran from giving away assets to family members, trusts, or other entities. Moreover, there are no written laws that create a penalty period of ineligibility for veteran benefits when and if a veteran has given away assets. Due to the lack of legal prohibition, many veterans have used various legal and financial strategies, within current laws, to reduce their assets, with varying results of success. Some of those strategies include:

1. transfer/gift assets to other family members
2. transfer/gift asset to specific types of trusts
3. utilize specific kinds of annuities
4. employ family members to provide care under a health-care contract

To reduce the incidences of involuntary impoverishment, the VA has proposed to implement a penalty period of ineligibility for any applicant who transfers assets or purchases an annuity. The VA will look back three years from the date of the application for any such transfers. The penalty of ineligibility, on the other hand, can be up to as much as 10 years. Although that may seem harsh, the real severity of the proposed change is that all gifts, to include gifts to charity, are presumed to have been given in order to qualify for the pension benefit, and thus, deny the application.

It is extremely difficult, if not impossible, for a veteran to be able to successfully appeal such a decision. The veteran would need to show by clear and convincing evidence that the transfer was the result of fraud, misrepresentation, or unfair business practices related to sale of financial products (annuities) or services for the purpose of obtaining VA benefits.

If the veteran and/or the veteran's family wanted to try to cure the penalty, it could be done only in the following manner:

1. all assets previously transferred must be returned within 30 days of filing the VA application;
2. evidence of the returned assets must be provided to the VA within 60 days from the time of the VA denial decision; and
3. no partial cures are allowed so as to shorten the time of the penalty.

Whether or not the penalty is cured, one question is, "how long is the penalty?" We already know that it can be as much as a 10-year period. However, it may also be a shorter period. The VA will take the value of the assets transferred and divide into that the maximum monthly pension rate with aid and attendance for the type of applicant.

For example, if a single veteran transfers $100,000 to a family member, the VA would divide $100,000 by $1,830, which would create a 54 month penalty period of ineligibility. If a married veteran transferred the same $100,000, his penalty divisor would be $2,169, creating only a

46-month penalty. The harshest penalty is to that of a widow, who transfers the same $100,000 with a penalty divisor of $1,176, creating a penalty period of 85 months.

Another significant proposed change is that the VA wants to clarify what is defined as a medical expense that would be deductible from the veteran's income, so as to qualify for any of its needs programs. Currently, all home health-care expenses, assisted living facility expenses, and nursing home expenses are 100 percent deductible from countable income. Moreover, expenses related to independent living facilities are also deductible if the applicant's physician certifies that the veteran must live there as it is a safe environment and that a third party, other than the independent living facility, is providing assistance with activities of daily living.

The clarification by the VA is the definition of Activities of Daily Living (ADLs). Those activities would be defined as dressing, bathing, toileting/incontinence, transferring, and eating. A new category would be added called "Instrumental Activities of Daily Living" (IADLs). Those would include such things as medication administration and the ability to use a phone. The last new category would be "Custodial Care" which would be defined as "needing assistance with two Activities of Daily Living OR assistance because of a mental disorder for a person who is unsafe if left alone due to that mental disorder."

Unfortunately for those veterans who are living in independent living facilities, the VA intends to disallow the deduction of payments for independent living facilities altogether and never deducted expenses related to Instrumental Activities of Daily Living.

Moreover, with regard to home health-care expenses, the VA intends to cap the deductible hourly rate at the national average of no more than $21.

At the time of publishing, the above proposed changes have not yet been implemented into law. Even so, veterans and their families are strongly advised to govern themselves in accordance with the proposed rules. It would be very unwise at this time to knowingly make asset transfers prior to the filing of a VA claim, unless doing so with the advice and supervision of an estate planning or elder care attorney who is accredited by the VA.

Where does this leave you? It has long been our recommendation to those in the community and long-term disease support groups that once a person is diagnosed with any degenerative disease or illness, they should begin to seek professional advice regarding governmental benefits. These days, a diagnosis of Alzheimer's disease, Parkinson's disease, or other dementia-producing diseases has a multiple-year trajectory. The sooner you get advice, the sooner you can use legal strategies to protect assets.

Experienced elder law estate planners can provide a panoramic and chronological viewpoint in which to make decisions that will allow legally permissible asset protection and, when appropriate, qualify a veteran or the widow(er) of a veteran for governmental long-term care benefits.

Governmental benefit-related asset protection is not a do-it-yourself project.

VA Benefits Checklist

Items you'll need depending upon whether you are a veteran, a veteran and spouse, or a widow/er of a veteran:

Veteran Only:

❑ DD-214 or Discharge Papers

❑ Annual Social Security Award Letter received in January OR other documentation to verify your income

❑ A printout from your pharmacy of 12 months of expenses

❑ Copies of all your latest financial statements

❑ Health insurance premiums and all other health related expenses

Veteran and Spouse:

All of the above for you and your spouse, PLUS

❑ Marriage certificate

❑ Death certificate or divorce decree if either spouse was previously married

❑ Health insurance premiums and all other health related expenses

Widow/er of Veteran:

- ❑ The veteran's DD-214 or Discharge Papers

- ❑ Annual Social Security Award Letter received in January AND other documentation to verify your income

- ❑ A printout from your pharmacy of three months of expenses

- ❑ Marriage certificate

- ❑ Veteran's death certificate

- ❑ Death certificate or divorce decree related to any previous marriages of either you or the veteran

- ❑ Copies of all your latest financial statements

- ❑ Health insurance premiums and all other health related expenses

Additional forms that will need to be filled out and filed with the claim for benefits:

- ❑ VA Form 21-2680—Statement of Attending Physician

- ❑ VA Form 21-0779—Nursing Home Information Report OR Care Provider Report

- ❑ Authorizations and Consent to Release Information to the VA for each physician of the veteran or spouse

- ❑ VA Form 8416 Medical Expense Report

Listing of Many VA Deductible Medical Expenses

These can be deducted from your gross income to determine VA benefit eligibility.

Medicare Premiums deducted from Social Security

Supplementary medical insurance (Part B) under Medicare

Abdominal supports

Acupuncture service

Ambulance hire

Anesthetist

Arch supports

Artificial limbs

Back supports

Braces

Cardiographs

Chiropodist

Chiropractor

Convalescent home (for medical treatment only)

Crutches

Dental services

Dentures

Dermatologist

Eyeglasses

Food or beverages prescribed by doctor for treatment of illness

Gynecologist

Hearing aids & batteries

Home health services

Hospital expenses

Insulin Treatment

Insurance premiums (medical)

Invalid chair

Lab tests

Lip reading lessons (in connection with disability)

Neurologist

Nursing services

Occupational therapist

Ophthalmologist

Optician

Optometrist

Oral surgery

Osteopath

Pediatrician

Physical examinations

Physician

Physical Therapy

Podiatrist

Prescriptions and drugs

Psychiatrist

Psychoanalyst

Psychologist

Psychotherapy

Radium therapy

Sacroiliac belt

Seeing-eye dog

Speech therapist

Splints

Surgeon

Telephone/teletype for deaf

Transportation expenses (20 cents per mile)

Vaccines

Vitamins prescribed by doctor

Wheelchairs

Whirlpool baths for medical purposes

X rays

Note: Most medical expenses must be prescribed by a physician to be deductible from gross income for VA benefit qualification purposes.

In addition to active duty vets from the armed services, these little-known groups also meet the active duty qualification for VA benefits. If you belong to any of these groups and received a discharge by the Secretary of Defense, your service meets the active duty service requirement for benefits:

- Recipients of the Medal of Honor
- Women Air Force Service Pilots (WASPs)
- Women's Army Auxiliary Corps (WAAC)
- Civilian employees of Pacific naval air bases who actively participated in defense of Wake Island during WWII
- Male civilian ferry pilots
- Wake Island defenders from Guam
- Civilian personnel assigned to OSS secret intelligence
- Guam Combat Patrol
- Quartermaster Corps members of the Keswick crew on Corregidor during WWII
- U.S. civilians who participated in the defense of Bataan
- U.S. merchant seamen who served on block ships in support of Operation Mulberry in the WWII invasion of Normandy
- American merchant marines in oceangoing service during WWII
- U.S. civilians of the American Field Service who served overseas under U.S. armies and U.S. army groups in WWII
- U.S. civilian employees of American Airlines who served overseas in contract with the Air Transport Command between 12/14/41 and 8/14/45
- Civilian crewmen of certain U.S. Coast and Geodetic Survey vessels between 12/7/41 and 8/15/45

- Members of the American Volunteer Group (Flying Tigers) who served between 12/7/41 and 8/14/45

- U.S. civilian flight crew and aviation ground support of TWA who served overseas between 12/14/41 and 8/14/45

- U.S. civilian flight crew and aviation ground support of Consolidated Vultee Aircraft Corp. who served overseas between 12/14/41 and 8/14/45

- Honorably discharged members of the American Volunteer Guard, Eritrea Service Command, between 6/21/42 and 3/31/43

- U.S. civilian flight crew and aviation ground support of Northwest Airlines who served overseas between 12/14/41 and 8/14/45

- U.S. civilian female employees of the U.S. Army Nurse Corps who served in the defense of Bataan and Corregidor from 1/2/42 to 2/3/45

- U.S. civilian flight crew and aviation ground support of Braniff Airways who served overseas in the North Atlantic between 2/26/42 to 8/14/45

- Chamorro and Carolina former native police who received military training in the Donnal area of central Saipan and were placed under command of Lt. Casino of the 6th Provisional Military Police Battalion to accompany U.S. Marines on active, combat patrol from 8/19/45 to 9/2/45

- The operational Analysis Group of the Office of Scientific Research and Development, Office of Emergency Management, which served overseas with the U.S. Army Air Corps from 12/7/41 through 8/15/45

- Honorably discharged members of the Alaska Territorial Guard during WWII

CHAPTER 9

GUARDIANSHIP AND CONSERVATORSHIP: OUT OF CONTROL AND FIGHTING BACK! THE LEGAL TOOLS TO REGAIN CONTROL AND STOP THE CHAOS

Real-Life Story: Circling Schemers

An elderly woman (we'll call her Mrs. West) was in the throes of a "casual care" relationship when referred to us as a possible guardianship candidate. "Casual care" refers to the complex web of neighbors, acquaintances, service providers, and others who occupy the periphery of a person's life and then gradually (or suddenly) find a pivotal role for themselves in the care and oversight of a vulnerable person. They appear to be well-meaning, sincere, and good-hearted, but they are not.

Mrs. West and her husband were very comfortable financially with assets in the area of $20 million, and they had established a solid estate plan. However, when Mr. West died, Mrs. West's world spun in an unexpected orbit.

Mr. West had always taken care of their finances. Tackling this unknown and unsavory job in her 80s was not an appealing proposition for Mrs. West.

The situation was made even worse by Mrs. West's situational depression following her husband's unexpected death, and the mild dementia she was hoping no one had noticed over the past couple of years. That dementia was stopping her from developing new skills. Even if she had an interest in juggling the details of her $20 million estate, her dementia would have precluded the acquisition of these new skills.

Mrs. West had a number of financial professionals charged with managing her estate. Sadly, it was one of these financial representatives who let her down first. His fees for managing her IRAs had run about $5,000 annually before Mr. West died. In the first year after Mr. West's death, those fees spiked to a shocking $150,000. While it's entirely possible there was a bit of extra management needed in those post-mortem months, an increase of this magnitude is strongly suggestive of opportunism. Mrs. West's ability to recognize the irregularity of a staggering fee hike was clouded by her depression and growing dementia.

The next person to see Mrs. West's situation as an opportunity to enrich themselves was the relative of a neighbor. She had heard just enough to understand that a lonely, grieving, and slightly demented, but very rich woman might appreciate some company. She might even appreciate it so much she would pay for it. Maybe she would even add her to the will!

The neighbor's relative started showing up a lot to visit Mrs. West. She played the role of a close and dear friend whose every moment was consumed with the comfort and well-being of Mrs. West.

The new friend ("Betty") ingratiated herself initially by offering to help around the house and shop for groceries. There were probably a lot of conversations over coffee as groceries were dropped off and the garden was tended, and Mrs. West quickly warmed to the idea of having someone fussing over her with great regularity.

Betty offered to help Mrs. West with all the complicated and pesky property and money and management. She put her name on a $300,000 bank account as co-owner with Mrs. West. She became power of attorney. Betty began to systematically terminate long-standing relationships with financial professionals and institutions. In the end, this greed was Betty's undoing.

The trust officers who had dutifully and honorably served Mrs. West for 20 years did not merely stand by and allow this new best friend to unravel Mrs. West's estate plan. They decided to stop Betty by pursuing guardianship.

The longtime trust officers brought the matter to the guardianship court for assessment of Mrs. West's competencies and protection of her person and assets. Mrs. West went through a battery of tests and was diagnosed with moderate dementia and depression. It was determined that she was not able to manage her finances but should participate in her personal life choices. A third-party guardian was appointed to sort out the web of intrigue that surrounded this gentle woman.

The guardian sifted through the rubble of Betty's activities. The $300,000 bank account that Betty put her name on as co-owner was returned to its prior sole owner, Mrs. West. The new will Betty had overseen, and the relocation of the trusts to new financial institutions, was determined by the court to have been done after Mrs. West lost her testamentary capacity. The original will and financial planning was thus honored. Mrs. West was provided professional caregivers that came from a licensed, bonded, and insured agency.

Now, Mrs. West lives in her home with a 24-hour caregiver. She travels weekly to the college where she used work to attend lectures and remain a part of the professional community that was her family. The guardian serves as insulation from professional opportunists that recognize her vulnerability. Without the protection of a guardian, her world would predictably remain in a helter-skelter pattern, and the financial investments would fill the pockets of the circling schemers who prey on the vulnerable.

117

Guardianship is designed to protect those who are overwhelmed due to age-related frailties, disabilities, or injuries. The goal is to maximize independence but also to protect and proactively prevent exploitation. Mrs. West is living in the community, using her resources to enhance her person-centered care plan as she ages in safety.

Now that the era of casual care has ended, Mrs. West is thriving in a structured setting, and her plan, as designed by her and her husband, is back on track.

To-Do Checklist

- ❑ Know what a guardianship is and what a guardian does
- ❑ Understand your loved one's current estate plan and be aware their needs may change
- ❑ Keep tabs on your loved one's Mental Capacity
- ❑ Understand the different types of guardianships and determine which might be the best fit
- ❑ Be aware of the reporting requirements for guardians in your state
- ❑ Know how (and when) to terminate/remove a guardian
- ❑ Determine if divorce is an option

Guardianship (or Conservatorship) to the Rescue

A **guardianship** is a legal relationship that is established and monitored by state courts and state laws. It is a way of empowering someone (the **guardian**) to act on behalf of an incapacitated individual (the **ward**).

In the case of estate planning for an individual with Alzheimer's disease, guardianships are usually a last resort. Unfortunately, if you have a loved one suffering from Alzheimer's and proper planning was not done before their **capacity** became diminished—that last resort will become a necessity.

"Capacity" generally means the mental ability to perceive and appreciate relevant facts, to understand the consequences of those facts, and to make rational decisions. "Incapacity" or "diminished capacity," then, describes the lack of those abilities.

Please be aware that each state has its own rules, and procedures for initiating guardianships for managing the personal and financial affairs of adults with disabilities or who are incapacitated. The terminology associated with these legal relationships varies a bit by state. Some states use the terms guardian and **conservator** interchangeably while some states use the term guardian to refer to a guardian of the person, and conservator to apply to a guardian of the estate. It is important that you find an elder law attorney to help you understand how your state works.

Whatever term a state uses, the purpose of the guardianship or **conservatorship** is to ensure the financial and personal well-being of adults who are incapacitated or have disabilities.

States tend to impose the least restrictive guardianship or conservatorship possible to maintain the well-being of the incapacitated person to preserve as many rights of the incapacitated person as possible.

Guardianship versus Powers of Attorney

An agent under a power of attorney trumps a guardian with respect to the exercise of any powers covered by the power of attorney. This is because courts defer to the agent who was nominated by the person with alleged disabilities at a time when the person was not under a disability and still had the capacity to appoint the agent.

Guardian Defined

A **guardian** is someone appointed by the court to serve as a representative of the person with a **legal disability**—for purposes of this book, Alzheimer's disease or another form of dementia. There are several definitions of "legal disability" and you need to know how your state defines the term when applying for a guardianship. For example, a severe loss in memory—brought on by Alzheimer's—can support a finding that an individual is disabled and unable to manage personal affairs in many states.

In most states, an individual may be adjudged to have a disability by a court after a competency hearing. If the individual is determined to be disabled, the court may appoint a guardian to promote the well-being of the disabled individual, to protect the individual, and to encourage development of his maximum self-reliance and independence.

Real-Life Story: Age, by Itself, Is Not a Disability

Some people find themselves the subject of guardianship proceedings because their conduct is somewhat contrary to our natural norms of society.

A 96-year-old man wanted to go to Las Vegas and marry his much younger, and very attractive, caregiver. This man was very wealthy and had not known his caregiver very long. Some of his family members questioned whether he was competent and started a guardianship proceeding to try to stop him from marrying the woman.

The judge agreed that it was a stupid decision to marry the caregiver; however, the judge ruled that this man was competent enough to make stupid decisions. The man did not need a guardian and was free to make bad personal decisions.

A court-appointed guardian has the authority to make decisions for the person with Alzheimer's without a court's involvement, provided the decisions are consistent with the procedures and requirements of the governing state. Guardians typically must provide periodic accounting to the court to ensure this consistency.

One of the authors, Kerry Peck, notes that, "Competent people are allowed to make stupid decisions, and we hear judges say that on a pretty regular basis."

Ask "Orientation Questions"

If you suspect a loved one's capacity may be diminishing, it is a good idea to ask them some "**orientation questions**." Orientation questions are simply questions to see if the individual can understand the time and the place they are in, who they are, and what's going on currently in the world.

Basic orientation questions would be asking individuals their address, how many children they have, their age, their name, and, if they are old enough, about their grandchildren.

It is also good to ask about current events. Is there a presidential election coming up? Who are the candidates? Is there some major world event, a hurricane that has occurred? Where did it occur?

You can also check your loved one's accuracy in sequencing various events in their own lives.

The answers to the orientation questions will give you a good jumping-off point, but you will need a medical expert to examine the individual to be absolutely sure when it comes to issues of dementia.

One of the key things you should do is bring in clinical professionals when your "gut" tells you something is not quite right with a loved one. It is not unusual for an individual with dementia to fool people into thinking they have capacity because they can act socially appropriate. They can work their way through a situation and seem totally normal, but if you ask the right questions and they don't have the mental flexibility to answer them perfectly, then a bona fide doubt exists.

Current Estate Plan

As soon as you learn that a loved one has Alzheimer's, you need to examine their current estate plan. If the individual has a well-drafted **power of attorney** or **living will**, they are in good shape. (See Chapter 4 for a description of powers of attorney and living wills.)

However, most individuals are not well prepared for the unexpected and do not have a power of attorney or living will. In these situations, you may need to turn to a guardianship.

Mental Capacity

Capacity is not an all-or-nothing concept. Capacity runs along a continuum and may vary according to several factors, such as the time of day, the task presented, and life stressors.

You should keep in mind that even when a loved one has Alzheimer's, they may still have valid preferences when they apparently cannot think clearly about complicated matters.

If a person is determined to be incompetent, another hearing will be held and the court will appoint a conservator to handle the individual's financial affairs and/or a guardian will be appointed to tend to their personal and health-care needs.

It is important to keep in mind that even though a person has Alzheimer's, that person's abilities and wishes should be honored as long as possible. Just because the individual is diagnosed with dementia does not mean that they lose all rights at the point of diagnosis.

The individual's competency may need to be determined, but a diagnosis of Alzheimer's does not instantly signal that a person is totally incapacitated. Dementia, like some other mental disorders, is progressive and degenerative. Professional evaluation is necessary to determine a person's competencies as they change over the trajectory of the disease.

You do need to be aware that when people with Alzheimer's lose the ability to make decisions for themselves; it will be absolutely necessary to have a guardian to legally make the decisions for them, if the proper planning was not put in place earlier.

Substituted Judgment Standard

When a guardian makes decisions on behalf of a ward, they should try and make the decisions as closely as possible to what the ward would have done or wanted under the circumstances. The guardian must consider the ward's personal, philosophical, religious and moral beliefs, and ethical values relative to the decision to be made by the guardian. Whenever possible, the guardian should determine how the ward would have made a decision based on the ward's previously expressed preferences, and make decisions in accordance with the preferences of the ward.

It is important to note that the "**substituted judgment**" refers to the preferences of the ward that were "previously expressed" (i.e., before the ward became incompetent). The ward's *current* desire, even if clearly and consistently expressed over the course of the proceedings, does not automatically trump all other considerations.

Estate Planning Problems

If a person with Alzheimer's is incapable of executing powers of attorneys or other estate- planning documents, it will become necessary to create a guardianship to transfer the assets of the individual with Alzheimer's. However, this leads to some problems:

- A guardianship adds time, expense and uncertainty to any proposed transfers of assets from the ward to their spouse and/or child with a disability.

- Guardians may not be authorized to make gifts in the same manner as would be possible through powers of attorney signed while a person is still mentally capable.

Conflict

In Alzheimer's cases, it is almost inevitable that the medical interests of the individual with disabilities and the financial interests of the heirs will conflict. The more money spent on caretaking, the less there will be left to inherit. An objective third party can always be appointed guardian to avoid family conflict.

Consider Hiring Professional Care Managers

Care managers are licensed clinical professionals usually with advanced degrees, with extensive knowledge of health care, aging, and different issues that affect people with disabilities, such as nurses, social workers, and licensed clinical counselors. They understand the health-care system and they know the right people to contact for specialized services.

When families are fighting over decisions to be made for/about their loved one, it helps to have a lawyer who can take a step back and make an independent judgment rather than relying on what they are told by the family. Family members can be very convincing in telling lawyers how much they care about the relative in question, but sometimes they are really more interested in the money. Some of the issues that are the most difficult arise when there are multiple marriages and multiple sets of children. There is often a preexisting conflict in those sets of children, and lawyers need to have great caution in counseling and representing them.

Types of Guardianships

Most states treat guardianships similarly, but often have slight variations, so it is important that you become familiar with your state's laws or contact an elder law attorney who is.

Generally, if a court determines a person has a disability, the court may appoint (1) a guardian of person, if it has been properly shown that because of the disability the person lacks sufficient understanding or capacity to make or communicate responsible decisions concerning the care of the person. Similarly, the court may appoint (2) a guardian of the estate (conservator), if it has been properly demonstrated that because of the disability the person is unable to manage his or her estate or financial affairs. Finally, a court may appoint (3) a guardian of person and the estate if that is what the individual needs.

Guardianships should only to be used as necessary to promote the well-being of the person with disabilities. That can mean to protect the person from neglect, exploitation, or abuse and to encourage the development of their maximum self-reliance and independence. Courts will only order a guardianship to the extent necessitated by the individual's actual mental, physical, and adaptive limitations.

The three main types of guardianships are the **plenary guardianship**, the **limited guardianship**, and the **temporary guardianship**.

A plenary guardianship is a guardianship in which the court gives the guardian the power to exercise all legal rights and duties for the ward, after the court finds the ward to be incapacitated. The two main subsets of plenary guardianships are **guardians of the person** and **guardians of the estate**.

Guardian of the Person

Typically, the guardian of the person may:

- make medical decisions;
- oversee the residential placement of their ward (with approval of the court);
- ensure that the ward receives proper professional services; and
- release medical records and information.

The guardian of the person should help the ward develop his or her maximum self-reliance and independence.

The guardian of the person may periodically request (or petition) the court to issue an order directing the guardian of the estate to pay the guardian of the person for the provision of the services. These payments would be strictly specified by the court order.

Surrogate Decision Maker

One reason that it is important to create a guardianship is to avoid having a **surrogate decision maker** assigned. While the courts will try to assign someone with the individual's best interests at heart, it does not always work out that way.

For example, if an incapacitated patient is in the hospital and does not have a living will or a power of attorney, the attending physician may appoint a surrogate decision maker who would then be authorized to make health-care decisions for the patient. These decisions include whether to forgo life-sustaining treatment. The order of priority for being appointed a surrogate decision maker varies from state to state but is generally:

1. the patient's guardian of the person;
2. the patient's spouse;
3. any adult child of the patient;
4. either parent of the patient;
5. any adult sibling of the patient;
6. any adult grandchild of the patient;
7. a close friend of the patient;
8. the patient's guardian of the estate.

Guardian of the Estate

The guardian of the estate (or conservator in some states) may generally do the following for the ward:

- make financial decisions;
- enter into contracts;
- estate planning;
- file lawsuits;
- sell real estate; and
- apply for government benefits.

The guardian has a **fiduciary duty** to investigate and pursue eligibility for government benefits to conserve the ward's estate assets. A fiduciary duty is a legal obligation to act in the best interest of another.

In cases involving substantial assets, the court may require (or the family or the parties may request) a corporate guardian of the estate. Just about all major banks, and many of the mid-tier banks, have trust departments that can act as guardian of the estate. However, a bank will not act as guardian of the person.

The guardian of the estate is responsible for the care, management, and investment of the estate to the extent specified in the court order establishing the guardianship. You should note that some states call a guardian of the estate a conservatorship. These terms can be used interchangeably and that can be confusing.

The guardian of the estate must manage the estate frugally and apply the income and principal of the estate so far as necessary for the comfort and suitable support of the ward, his minor and adult dependent children, and persons related by blood or marriage who are dependent upon or entitled to support from the ward. The guardian may make disbursement payments of the ward's funds and estate directly to the ward or other dependents as directed by the court.

Short-Term Guardian

A guardian of a person may appoint a short-term guardian to take over the guardian's duties, each time the guardian is unavailable or unable to carry out those duties. Some states require this to be done in writing, but may not require court approval. Others may require a court to sign off on the assignment. Be sure to have your elder law attorney check the rules for your state if you need a short-term guardian.

The (permanent) guardian should consult with the ward, when possible, to determine a preference concerning the person to be appointed as short-term guardian, and the guardian should give proper consideration to that preference in choosing a short-term guardian.

Temporary Guardian

There are certain circumstances, like a guardian's death, incapacity, or resignation, in which the court may need to appoint a temporary guardian. Sometimes the temporary guardian is referred to as a **Guardian Ad Litem**. For a temporary guardian to be appointed, it must be considered necessary for the immediate welfare and protection of the person (ward) or their estate.

In determining the necessity for temporary guardianship, the immediate welfare and protection of the person and estate must be of paramount concern. The interests of any interested person, any care provider, or any other party may not outweigh the interests of the ward. The temporary guardian will have all of the powers and duties that the guardian of the person or of the estate had. Generally, the court order creating a temporary guardian must state the actual reason identified by the court that necessitates the temporary guardianship.

Real-Life Story: Temporary Guardianship Cases Are Emergency Situations

A lawyer was appointed guardian ad litem in a temporary guardianship case in which the children couldn't agree whether their mother should have neurosurgery. The court ordered that the hearing occur the same day as it was filed. The guardian ad litem was directed to go out and talk to the doctors, examine the records, and come back and make a report to the court.

This is an extreme example, but time is of the essence in temporary guardianship situations.

In almost every scenario involving Alzheimer's disease, the family filing for guardianship of their loved one wants a full plenary guardian. However, they may also have a need to file a temporary guardianship. The need for a temporary guardianship for someone suffering from

Alzheimer's disease typically occurs in instances of financial exploitation. (See Chapter 10 for more information on financial exploitation.)

A guardian ad litem is often referred to as the eyes and ears of the court. In most states, the court appoints a guardian ad litem to visit the person being considered for a temporary guardianship and make a determination. The guardian ad litem then reports back to the court and gives an opinion as to whether emergency relief is necessary and reasonable under the circumstances.

This is done before the actual temporary guardianship hearing.

Real-Life Story: The Neglectful Agent

A charitable group contacted a professional care manager about an elderly immigrant with Alzheimer's disease who needed help because the woman's agents under her powers of attorney were not acting on her behalf.

The woman did not have adequate food and was literally starving. She was giving all her money away to her neighbors. She had a caregiver, but the caregiver was an addict who kept taking the woman to the emergency room to get Tylenol with codeine and taking it all herself.

The woman had congestive heart failure that was not being treated. She had pain that was not being treated. She had oxygen tanks, but they were all empty. The powers of attorney would not help her. They were located two states away and would not provide any service for her because they thought she was fine.

The care managers were able to be named temporary guardians and were able to provide caregivers. Fortunately, the care managers were able to inform the woman's family. The family finally realized that if they did not step up to the plate and do the job, somebody else would and they would lose control.

One of the family members actually moved in with the woman and became her caregiver. The elderly woman was able to stay in her own home with care, and the care managers turned the guardianship over to the family with court supervision.

This is an example of excellent work by a lawyer who knows the system, knows the preference of the court to have family manage things. But if the family is not doing a good job, then they start getting supervised by the court because the courts are going to protect the person with disabilities.

That's the role of a good guardianship lawyer. Once the guardianship process is in place, the least restricted environment principle needs to apply, but sometimes it takes an iron fist to ensure the family does a good job.

Typically, the steps for obtaining (petitioning for) a temporary guardianship are:

Step 1: Obtain a physician's report and file the appropriate court form(s). The report must be completed by a physician (M.D. or D.O.). The Physician's Report should include:

- a diagnosis that the respondent (person who needs the guardianship) suffers from one of the following is partially or totally incapable of making personal or financial decisions:
  - mental deterioration
  - physical incapacity
  - mental illness
  - developmental disability
- a description of the nature and type of person's disability;
- how the disability affects the patient's functioning and decision-making;
- an analysis of the results of evaluations of the person's mental and physical condition;
- information on educational condition, adaptive behavior, and social skills;
- whether the person is in need of a guardian and the type and scope of the guardianship needed;
- a recommendation of the most suitable living arrangement for the person.

Step 2: You should file petitions for plenary and temporary guardianship simultaneously.

- The temporary guardianship petition must state why a temporary guardian is necessary.
- Focus on "the immediate welfare and protection of the alleged disabled person and/or his estate."

Step 3: After filing the temporary guardianship petition, a guardian ad litem must be appointed.

Temporary Guardianship Powers

Remember that a temporary guardian is authorized to have all the listed powers and duties available to a plenary or "full-time" guardian. Therefore, it is imperative to carefully detail any and all powers sought in the temporary petition.

Real-Life Story: Guardian Ad Litem

A lawyer was appointed guardian ad litem in a case in which the son of the person with alleged disabilities had filed a court order seeking to remove his father's life support. The lawyer was told that the patient was in a deep coma and was dying from lung cancer. The court directed the lawyer to go investigate the situation on a very expedient basis and then return for a hearing.

After spending hours with the doctors and medical team, the lawyer then went in and attempted to communicate with the person. The lawyer got down and spoke very loudly into the patient's ear (the patient was wearing an oxygen mask) and told the patient the reason for his visit. The patient promptly sprung up out of bed, used a variety of profanities relative to his son and indicated that he was sure his son had come to town to get his money because he hadn't seen him in about 10 years.

The fact that the third-party guardian ad litem was able to go and advise this man of the existence of this case against him to remove life support, and the fact that it worked because he obviously opposed the removal of life support shows the importance of guardian ad litems and their role of protecting people's rights. This man was on the verge of being taken advantage of, and in essence losing his life.

Temporary guardianships are by definition, temporary. Typically, they expire within 60 days. Extensions are normally not granted, but can be in some situations.

Limited Guardianship

In cases of limited guardianships, a limited guardian is appointed and charged with taking away certain rights of an individual and giving certain rights. For example, the person with diminished capacity may lose the right to contract, but may retain the right to receive $500 a month of personal discretionary spending money.

Limited Guardianships May Cause Trouble Down the Line

Sometimes families may attempt to settle a guardianship dispute before trial by agreeing to the appointment of a limited guardian of the disabled person, estate, or both. This may seem like a good compromise and a way to avoid family strife, but practically speaking, appointing a limited guardian can pose problems in the future. For example, for a person with a diagnosis of progressive dementia, the duties and powers of the guardian and the legal disabilities that must be included in the limited guardian order will change over time based on the very nature of the person's disability.

The duties and powers of the limited guardian must be specifically laid out in the court order to distinguish between the authority of the limited guardian and the powers retained by your affected loved one. Therefore, your lawyer may be forced to go into court on multiple occasions to modify the terms of the limited guardianship as the loved one's disability progresses.

Get Court Authority for Legal Action

The guardian should always ask for court authority to begin, prosecute, or defend any legal action on behalf of the ward. After appointment, all legal matters and proceedings on behalf of the ward should be brought by the guardian in the capacity as guardian, rather than in the name of the person with disabilities. The guardian of the estate may settle any lawsuit involving the ward, but the probate court must first approve settlement as in the best interests of ward.

Many people do not realize that protective orders can be issued from the guardianship court. The purpose of a guardianship is to guard and protect. You need to be aware of all the available tools to guard and protect your loved one and their assets. If you have hired a competent elder law attorney, you are likely already aware of this or your attorney is handling this for you.

Reporting Requirements

There are some general reporting requirements that go along with guardianships. These requirements are set by the states and are pretty similar, but there are bound to be some differences, so you should consider hiring a lawyer who is familiar with the requirements of your state.

Real-Life Story: Emergencies

A care manager was notified of an elderly woman who was living alone. This woman was suffering from a lot of physical deficits and allegedly had two bad sons. A lawyer presented the case to the court as an emergency because one of the sons was a convicted felon who was getting out of jail in three days and was going to move back in with his mother. In the past, the son prevented his mother from getting any care because he would threaten her caregivers with violence.

The woman had a slight case of Alzheimer's and a fierce loyalty to her son and insisted that her son was fine and wasn't causing problems. However, if the caregivers would all leave, it would put her in a dire situation. So, the lawyer's job was to go into court, get a temporary guardianship in place, and protect the woman by stopping the convicted felon son from moving back into her house.

The experienced lawyer on the case was able to present the urgency of moving forward and getting orders of protection through the guardianship court to protect this woman from the convicted felon. Checking past police reports, the lawyer found reports of 46 police visits to the home for violent episodes. These reports included domestic violence, violence against the neighbors, brandishing a butcher knife, and chasing caregivers around the apartment.

The woman had forgotten about these incidents due to her Alzheimer's. The lawyer was able to get an emergency guardianship in place within 24 hours. Professional caregivers were appointed to manage the care environment and care providers.

With the ex-con son out of the picture, the care managers discovered that the other son wasn't really a bad guy. It turned out that he was petrified of his brother and wouldn't go and help in the house when his brother was present because he feared for his safety. They were able to work with the other son, and the mother actually moved in with her "better son." A 24-hour caregiver was put in place to monitor the situation.

After a short period of time, it was prudent to pull out the 24-hour caregiver. The good son has been able to take care of his mother for the last two years. The other son is not disrupting the care anymore, and it's actually a very successful and economical outcome.

Guardian of Person

Generally, the guardian of the person must file a report with the court at the intervals indicated by the court. Typically, the report must briefly state:

1. the current mental, physical, and social condition of the ward and the ward's minor and adult dependent children;

2. the present living arrangement, and a description and the address of every residence where the guardian lived during the reporting period and the length of stay at each place;

3. a summary of the medical, educational, vocational, and other professional services given to the guardian;

4. a résumé of the guardian's visits with and activities on behalf of the ward and the ward's minor and adult dependent children;

5. a recommendation as to the need for continued guardianship;

6. any other information requested by the court or useful in the opinion of the guardian.

In most states, the guardian can ask the Office of the State Guardian to assist him or her in filing the report. The court is then authorized to review the report and take any actions it deems appropriate pursuant to the report.

Guardian of Estate

Most states require guardians of estate to file inventories of the ward's assets and periodic accounting of the estate receipts and disbursements. It is important to keep very detailed records of all disbursements and expenditures. A court can request to review any and all estate expenditures, and the guardian may be held accountable for estate assets improperly managed.

Picking the Guardian

It is crucial to examine the potential guardians' abilities and skill set when choosing a person to serve as guardian for your loved one. The correct choice may be a spouse, adult child, or friend. However, if there is no one in the person's life with the correct abilities and skill set, you need to consider other options.

Some states and/or counties have officials who serve as public guardians. Another option is private professional guardians certified by the National Guardianship Association, Inc. (www.guardianship.org).

It is unfortunate, but not unusual, for family members and friends to disagree about who should act as the person's guardian. In some cases, a lawyer may have to actually prove in court who should be the guardian. In these instances, the parties will frequently indicate that they're fighting for the loved one's medical care and control when they're really fighting for control of the money and how much is going to be spent on their loved one versus being part of their inheritance.

It is best to try to avoid a full-blown contested hearing to choose a guardian though. Many parties try to settle matters by agreeing to the appointment of financial institutions, geriatric care managers, county public guardians, or any other neutral party as guardian when family members and friends are contesting the choice of guardian. There are even some not-for-profit guardianship agencies that will act as guardian of the person and some of them act as both guardian of the estate and guardian of the person.

Termination/Removal of the Guardian

It is difficult to have a guardian removed for improper conduct unless there's a clear case of theft. You can get a guardian removed when you find out that the person who is the guardian is inappropriate or is making bad decisions, but it is a difficult and time-consuming task. It is really important that you get the correct person named as guardian to begin with. Otherwise you will potentially have a long court battle on your hands. If you find yourself in a situation where you need to have your loved one's guardian removed you should hire a competent elder law attorney to guide you through the legal process.

Divorce and Guardianship Issues for Individuals with Alzheimer's Disease

Guardians typically have the power to make personal decisions about their ward's health care, end-of-life treatment, place of residence, and visitors. However, one area that many states still find too personal to allow a guardian or conservator to act on behalf of the ward for—is divorce.

Most states will not allow guardians and conservators to bring a divorce action on behalf of a ward unless that state actually has a state law expressly allowing it. However, a growing minority of states are beginning to rule that a guardian or conservator can bring a divorce action on behalf of a ward even in the absence of state laws permitting such an action.

Divorce is frequently an economic issue, but it also comes up in scenarios in which the husband and wife has clearly drifted apart. Maybe one is living in a nursing home or long-term-care facility and the other is living in the community, it is quite rare that seniors with long-term marriage choose to divorce in this circumstance. If and when, a divorce is considered in this type of situation, it would be wise to consult with both an attorney focused in divorce (family law) and an elder law attorney.

Another thing to keep in mind is that, for Medicaid planning, sometimes it's important to consider a legal separation as opposed to a divorce. This is an area that your elder law attorney can help explain to you.

Sometimes people are opposed to a divorce for religious reasons, but they want to have a legal separation to get a court order on who retains what assets. (Medicaid planning is discussed in Chapter 6.) While divorce/separation is a very personal decision, it is something that you may need to consider in certain circumstances with Alzheimer's disease.

CHAPTER 10

STOP THE MONEY THIEVES! SCAMMERS, OPPORTUNISTS, AND FAMILY MEMBERS

Real-Life Story: Sex for Signatures

On a warm Friday afternoon in Chicago, a Baby Boomer son and daughter of a physically healthy 86-year-old man named Eugene sat across the desk from a respected and experienced elder law litigator. They had come to see the lawyer for advice regarding concerns they had about their father and his new friend Olga. This is the story they shared.

"Dad married his high school sweetheart—that was our mom, Doris. They were married for over 50 years. Mom and Dad were always devoted to each other. For many years Mom suffered from debilitating diabetes, and then cancer. Mom loved Dad with all her heart, but we know that she had been much too frail to have had a truly intimate relationship with him for a long, long time.

"Mom and Dad had always been very religiously conservative—but for the last fifteen years or so, Mom wasn't even able to attend church. After Mom's death, there was a funeral at the church. It seemed like everyone in the community turned out, because Mom and Dad were so respected. A woman named Olga, whom none of us had ever met before, attended the funeral. She warmly addressed all of the family members and expressed her condolences for our loss. She appeared to be about 65 years of age and fit as a fiddle.

(continued on the next page)

"After the funeral, Olga began attending church and all of the older adult activities. She publicly declared her faith and volunteered to help out wherever she was needed. After a while, people told us that everywhere that Dad went, Olga was sitting right beside him. I think our dad was quite flattered to have the attention of a younger woman, after all those years of caring for Mom. The relationship seems to have become romantic within a matter of months after Mom's funeral.

"We children had noticed that Dad was becoming 'a little forgetful,' but we considered that just a normal part of old age. Dad has always been close with all of us kids, and he told us about Olga. We were very happy for him to have a companion and to be getting out of the house.

Everything seemed to start out okay—but during the last few months Dad has become more withdrawn from family activities. He doesn't call or return calls like he used to. He stopped sending birthday cards to the grandkids (which always had a $50 bill in them). Some of us kids attempted a trip home to see Dad for Thanksgiving—but we were told quite bluntly, 'No, please don't come. I'm going to have Thanksgiving with Olga and her family.'

"Right after Thanksgiving we got a call from a lifelong family friend who is Dad's accountant. He urged us to visit Dad, because he had been visited by Dad and Olga. He indicated that substantial changes in ownership of assets were being discussed. He recommended that we contact you, Mr. Attorney."

After listening to this story, the wise yet cynical lawyer stated, "From my experience, this is possibly a case of professional financial exploitation—especially because your father perhaps suffers from a bit of dementia. You told me that most likely your father and mother had not been intimate for many years, and I think it's very probable that there is sexual activity going on between Olga and Eugene. I refer to this as the 'sex for signatures' scam."

Immediately the son and daughter stood up, outraged. "You have no business insulting our family and our father! Our dad has always been an upstanding man of the faith! I resent your comments and your lack of empathy!" After saying that, they promptly left the office.

On the following Monday morning, the first call into the lawyer's office was from the son and daughter, who had spent the weekend at their dad's house. As soon as the phone was answered, they said to the lawyer, "We can't believe it! You were right. During the weekend we heard the unmistakable sounds of intimacy coming from our father's room. And that's not the worst of it! There was a brand-new Lexus sitting in the driveway, for which Dad had cosigned the loan. But the car title is in Olga's name."

To-Do Checklist

- ❏ Be aware of the different types of financial exploitation

- ❏ Keep tabs on your loved one's advisors/guardian

- ❏ Look out for a new power of attorney or changes in an existing power of attorney

- ❏ Be on the lookout for new people who suddenly hold important roles in your loved one's life

Financial Exploitation

As you are probably aware, instances of financial exploitation are on the rise. Senior citizens are frequent targets for scammers. Sadly, about 90 percent of the financial exploitation of seniors is committed by family members or people that they should be able to trust, like caregivers.

Seniors, especially seniors with dementia, are the perfect victims because they generally won't report the abuse for a variety of reasons ranging from embarrassment to fear that if they turn in their relative or caregiver they will be put in a nursing home because there will be nobody left to care for them in their home.

The majority of these cases combine financial exploitation and emotional abuse. They go hand in hand, because an abuser will manipulate Mom or Dad's emotions to exploit money from them.

More often than not, these instances of money thievery involve some form of abuse of a **power of attorney**.

Real-Life Story: Financial Exploitation and Emotional Abuse

In a recent elder abuse case, the daughter constantly told her elderly mother, "You were never there for me as a child. You were a horrible mother. You never bought me the things that I wanted." The mother was suffering from dementia, and the daughter convinced her to sign paperwork giving the daughter power of attorney for financial matters.

Soon after the documents were signed, the daughter used her mother's funds to buy herself a vacation home in Florida. Likely, the daughter felt entitled to the vacation home.

Another situation that often leads to financial exploitation and emotional abuse is when adult children with drug or alcohol problems move into a parent's home. The children often end up living off of the parent and eventually become verbally abusive to get more money to purchase drugs or alcohol. In some cases, they will get their parent to sign documents giving them power of attorney in order to have easier access to money for drugs and alcohol.

Power of attorney documents are wonderful tools, but they can be problematic in the wrong situation. They are just too easy to fill in and forge, or to have somebody without **capacity** sign. Most outsiders will assume the powers of attorney are legitimate. They are probably one of the single most abused documents when it comes to financial exploitation.

Real-Life Story: Capacity Before Creating a Power of Attorney

It is so important to have a doctor examine a loved one if there might be any issue with capacity. Always err on the side of being overly cautious.

One of the challenges with some forms of dementia is that it is very hard for a non-medical professional to determine capacity, and even giving a **Mini-Mental State Exam** (**MMSE**) can still lead to a false conclusion that people have capacity—but in reality, they don't understand the consequences of their acts.

You should consider an elder law attorney who has experience in working with persons with capacity issues to draft the powers of attorney for your loved one. Many people treat powers of attorney as if they are an unimportant throwaway document—but in a senior's life (particularly one with dementia) it is not a throwaway document! In the wrong hands, it can empower somebody to have absolute license to steal.

Author Kerry Peck shares his thoughts on the dangers of the misuse of a power of attorney:

Unfortunately, when a **durable power of attorney for property** is signed inappropriately, it can be used on a regular basis

140

to exploit a senior. People no longer use guns to rob banks; today they use a durable power of attorney. A durable power of attorney, when presented to an unsuspecting teller of a bank, can be used to withdrawal massive sums of money.

Real-Life Story: The Crooked Family Lawyer and a Broad Power of Attorney

Susie never married or had children and ended up outliving all of her relatives. As various family members passed away, Susie inherited their estates. Susie's last living relative, her brother, died when she was 66. After inheriting her brother's estate, Susie had about $350,000 in investment accounts and owned her longtime home outright.

Susie needed these funds to last for the rest of her life. After her brother died, Susie had no family to look after her. When she reached her early 70s, Susie developed Alzheimer's disease and was soon unable to protect her interests. She began to rely more and more on the family's longtime, trusted lawyer to help her with finances. Susie was incapacitated, but the lawyer had her sign a very broad power of attorney agreement granting the lawyer virtually unfettered access to all of her money. Shortly after Susie signed the instrument, the lawyer started to plunder her funds.

Over an eight-year period, the lawyer stole $176,000 from Susie's accounts. He also squandered away large portions of Susie's pension and social security. When the lawyer had worked his way through Susie's savings and investment accounts, he sold her longtime home to his friend and client for far less than its market value. He then helped himself to much of the remaining sale proceeds.

After selling Susie's home, the lawyer moved her into a very small apartment on the other side of town, away from the neighborhood where she had lived her entire life. At this point, her old neighbors became suspicious and called the police, who referred the case to the Public Guardian Program. The Public Guardian subsequently became Susie's guardian and sued the lawyer for recovery of Susie's home and the funds he stole. They also reported him to the Attorney Registration and Disciplinary Commission. The case eventually settled, and Susie's house and her savings were returned to her. She was able to move back into her longtime home, where she lived out the remaining years of her life. The lawyer was disbarred.

Susie's story illustrates a common theme in many financial exploitation cases: the exploiter is often someone in a position of trust and authority who abuses this power for their own financial gain. While some cases involve strangers who exploit the vulnerable, the majority of cases involve people who are uniquely positioned to take advantage of the disabled person, such as **fiduciaries**, family members, and trusted members of society.

Another big issue in financial exploitation is the monitoring (or lack thereof) of legal **guardians**. If the guardian is financially exploiting the **ward**—who is looking out for the ward? In a perfect world, the court system is overseeing and monitoring the guardianship process, but that is often not the case in the real world.

Some courts do a great job monitoring guardians, but many do not. The courts that are doing a better job have mechanisms in place so that when a guardian does not file accounting paperwork, it sets off a red flag and a citation is sent to the guardian.

Clues to Financial Exploitation

Sometimes you need to do a little detective work on your own if your loved one has Alzheimer's disease and you are concerned that they are possibly being exploited. If you suspect that a loved one is the victim of embezzlement, one of the first things to look for when examining their financial records is large checks ending in all zeros—because real, typical checks that people write are for amounts more like $517.33 or something similar. So look for checks in even amounts like $2,500, $500, or $1,500. Those kinds of numbers are where to start looking to see if somebody is taking money.

Another thing to look for is the use of ATMs. Most elderly people do not use ATMs. They typically are more likely to go into the bank and deal with someone face to face. If there are suddenly a lot of ATM withdrawals, that should be a red flag.

Another red flag is if they are purchasing things that elderly people with dementia just don't normally buy. An 80-year-old person without a computer who doesn't drive anymore is not going to buy a BMW or make purchases from iTunes. You need to look at the person's spending and question if these types of expenditures make sense for somebody who's bedridden and 80- something, or whatever the fact pattern is.

Financial fraud may be experiencing an uptick, but many scams that are prevalent now are not new. Most online scams today are not that different than the scams run by the snake oil salesmen and con men of the 1800s.

Stranger Danger

Most money thieves are going to be people your loved one knows and trusts—but you also need to be aware of the professional scammers who will try to prey on your loved one. "Stranger danger" makes up only about 10 percent of the cases of financial exploitation, but these scammers are getting more and more sophisticated.

Just as seniors are easy prey for dishonest family members and caregivers, they are prime targets for criminals. Criminals see seniors as easy marks for financial scams for many of the same reasons as family and caregivers, but also because seniors are easy to reach:

- They can get to seniors on the phone. A lot of seniors are lonely, so they'll talk to a stranger on the phone. Elderly people will almost always answer the phone, even if the caller ID says Kingston, Jamaica.

- Criminals can get to seniors through the mail, too, because seniors tend to read every piece of mail front and back. They look forward to the mailman bringing them their mail! Studies have shown that seniors place unusually high validity in direct mail solicitations.

- Additionally, seniors are usually home a lot and tend to answer the door. This means that seniors are susceptible to financial exploitation scams over the phone, through the mail, and face to face.

- Many criminals and scam artists can spot a senior's home just by looking at it. Houses that have an American flag flying, a Buick in the driveway, and well-tended flowers are often owned by senior citizens. Bad guys from all over the world can target seniors using online maps and street views because of these distinctive features of homes owned by seniors.

Now add the fact that the senior might be suffering from dementia, and there's a lot of opportunity for criminals to financially exploit this group.

One of the most common tools being used by scammers today is the green dot MoneyPak. They are available for purchase at most big box stores and the card itself is perfectly legitimate. It is simply a card to put money on and then use it as a debit card of sorts. This card plays a large role in the "grandma scam" and many lottery scams.

The Grandma Scam

A common scam is for the thief to call an elderly woman and say, "Hi, Grandma, this is your granddaughter." The senior responds, "Oh—is this Kim?" Now the scammer has Grandma on the hook and can reel her in.

The scammer proceeds to tell the senior, "I am on my way to a wedding at Niagara Falls and I got into a car accident and I need money." Or "Grandma, I'm in jail and they got me for drug charges. But you know that doesn't sound like me! I got a cold—they guy next to me on the plane had a cold and I got it. So I took Nyquil and that's why I have drugs in my system. I need you to send money right away, Grandma."

The scammer then instructs the senior to get a green dot MoneyPak and put money on the card and to await a call back to get the card number.

If the senior pays the first time, the scammers will probably make up another reason that they need money and will continue to call and take the senior's money, until Grandma runs out of money or somebody figures out it's a scam.

Lottery Scam

The typical lottery scam works as follows: Seniors receive a call from outside the country and are told they won a foreign lottery. However, they have to prepay the taxes before the winnings can be released to them. The caller will tell them to go to Wal-Mart and pick up a green dot MoneyPak, place $500 on the card, and go back home to await the next phone call in an hour.

The scammer is attempting two things here. First, by sending the senior to a big box store, it is less likely that the senior will know the cashier and talk about the lottery winnings. Second, by saying he will call back in an hour, the caller is not giving the senior time to think clearly or talk to family about the phone call.

When the scammer calls back, he will have the senior read the 14-number code on the back of the MoneyPak. Once the scammer has the code, he has access to the money on the card and can steal it from the senior.

A variation of the lottery scam involves sending checks to seniors. The senior then tries to cash the check and the check bounces. The bounced check is returned to the scammer with the senior's bank account information on the check (and the senior is hit with a fee for the bounced check).

Spoofing

Another phone-related scam is called "spoofing." Spoofing is when a person knows how to change the incoming caller ID on calls they make to unsuspecting seniors. Sophisticated criminals can make the caller ID appear to be that of a bank's. Then they call up seniors and tell them that there is a problem with their account and ask them to verify their account number, etc. And soon enough, they have the senior's account information.

This can also be done by an email that appears to be from the bank requesting account information. Never give your bank account information out through an email or email link! Your real bank would not ask for such information through an email.

Ruse Entry

A ruse entry involves scammers faking their way into a senior's home for the purposes of robbing them. It works best if they can catch seniors out in the yard. They may tell them that they are new neighbors and ask if they could come into the backyard for just a couple of seconds and see the garden. What they're really doing is distracting the senior, and someone else is coming in the front door and going straight to the bedroom to steal whatever they can.

A variation of this scam is to claim they are from the city's water department and say they are down the street digging in the yards and they think they hit a water line. They just need to come in for one minute and check out the basement. They get the senior downstairs and run water and make noise. Meanwhile, the second guy is in the bedroom robbing the senior.

Drive-by Contractors

Another scam to be on the lookout for is the door-to-door contractor. For example, some men show up and claim to have just finished reroofing a garage down the street. They claim to have extra materials and offer the homeowner a great deal. If the homeowner accepts, they will try to get paid up front and then will either do shoddy work or start the job and then disappear.

You should advise your loved one to never respond to people who are soliciting them for business. Never use people who go door to door to ask to work on your house—contractors who have good business reputations don't go door to door—they have enough business as it is.

Stockbrokers who are making cold calls probably are not very good stockbrokers, even if they are honest. Never, ever respond to solicitations by e-mail, in person, or on the phone.

A big reason these scams work on seniors so often is because they are so trusting. Because they trust people, they don't want to say, "I don't know who you are. Where's your car? I don't see your vehicle. Let me see some identification." They don't want to say that to people because they'll think they'll offend them, so they won't ask—they'll just let them in their home.

There is also a fear of retaliation with elderly victims. Or there could be a fear of going to court and being unfamiliar with where to go and what to do. There could be a fear of being found unfit to live alone in their home and a fear of being put in a nursing home. However, the main reason most seniors don't want to contact the police is because they are embarrassed.

Some financial exploitation doesn't start out as a scam. Elderly individuals who are suffering from dementia who forget to pay their bills or taxes can also become victims of financial exploitation.

Unfortunately for many seniors who have lost their ability to handle their bills, legislators have put into place real estate tax and judgment creditor collection laws based on the assumption that the debtor has the legal capacity of a fully functional 30-year-old adult. Professional real estate tax and debt collection scavengers have developed profitable systems to acquire homes from the vulnerable.

146

Real-Life Story: Legally Protected Exploiters

Maxine was in the early stages of dementia. She owned a house with her husband and had lived in this house for 20 years. They owned the house outright. Maxine's husband always paid the bills and took care of the financial matters. Her husband died and her dementia worsened. At one point, the police found her wandering naked in the streets on a freezing January night.

Maxine was then put in a hospital instead of being returned to her home.

While she was hospitalized, Maxine's property taxes came due, and they were sold to a tax scavenger for nonpayment. The scavenger forced a tax deed sale of Maxine's home for the nonpayment of the taxes. The property taxes at issue amounted to less than $350! The notices of the tax deed sale were sent to Maxine's home, but she was residing at a state mental health hospital at the time. The mailman was aware of her hospitalization and returned the tax sale notices to the sender with the notation "Person is hospitalized" written on the envelopes.

No one ever contacted the mailman or anyone else at the post office about the returned envelopes. Even though the scavenger knew that the notices of the tax deed sale of Maxine's longtime home had been returned unserved and even though important clues as to Maxine's whereabouts were written on the faces of the returned envelopes, the scavenger proceeded with the forced tax lien sale and obtained a tax deed to Maxine's home.

The trial judge involved in the forced tax sale would later testify in an affidavit that if this information had been disclosed to him, he would not have approved the forced sale.

Shortly after the tax sale, the Office of the Public Guardian was appointed guardian on behalf of Maxine. Her guardian immediately moved to vacate the tax deed and argued that Maxine had never received the returned notices that she was about to lose her home due to unpaid taxes. The guardian also presented uncontroverted expert medical evidence that, even if Maxine had received the notices, she would not have been able to understand their import or act to protect herself, due to her mental illness and decline.

(continued on the next page)

The guardian further argued that the scavenger was obligated to follow up on the notations on the returned envelopes and that the notations on the returned notices, along with the fact that a valuable house with no mortgage, liens, or encumbrances was being lost over a mere $347 in unpaid taxes, put the scavenger on notice that something was amiss.

After a lengthy trial, the court denied the motion to vacate the tax deed. The court agreed that Maxine did not receive the notices. The court also agreed with the expert witness psychiatrist that, even if she had received the notices, Maxine would not have been able to understand their meaning or to act. However, the court held that, although the scavenger was on notice that Maxine was hospitalized, he was not on notice that she was hospitalized due to a mental disability.

In addition, the court ruled that the scavenger was under no legal obligation to follow up on the information on the returned notices.

Note: state laws vary regarding tax lien foreclosure

Vulnerability

A 2012 University of California–Los Angeles study conducted by Shelley E. Taylor, a distinguished professor of psychology, found that older people are more likely to fall for scams, because they are less likely to judge an untrustworthy face as a potentially dishonest person. (The study can be viewed at http://newsroom.ucla.edu/portal/ucla/why-older-adults-become-fraud-241076.aspx.) Apparently, this is because the portion of our brains that is linked to distrust and is important for recognizing untrustworthy faces, becomes less active as we age.

The study found that we start to lose the skills we need to make sound financial choices as early as our fifties! Not only is this fascinating, but it drives home the very important warning that seniors can be vulnerable to financial exploitation before the point at which they are legally incapacitated.

A majority of elderly fraud victims are suffering from some sort of vulnerability because of aging. Many times that vulnerability does not render the victim legally incapacitated.

Real-Life Story: Determination of Incapacity

One of the authors actually heard a physician say, "I would not determine a person to be incapacitated unless I was convinced that if there was a fire in their home, they would not know enough to leave."

This is troubling because people become vulnerable from a financial standpoint long before they would know to leave if the room were on fire! The author then asked the doctor, "What, if anything, could you do if a person was losing their ability but it hadn't reached the level of incapacity?"

The doctor replied: "Well, there's no Medicare reimbursement code for the determination of vulnerability. There's no protocol for vulnerability. I could not do anything."

Often the vulnerability is mental, but sometimes it is physical. Physical vulnerability doesn't just mean a physical disability that can be seen, but can mean the person can't do something that they used to be able to do, like get out and go to the bank themselves. Maybe there is vision loss and they have to have someone else sign checks. That vision loss opens up that door for someone else to take advantage of them without their ever knowing it.

It isn't always easy to notice the declining mental abilities of your loved one, because it is such a gray area. And some seniors are very good at hiding their decline.

Senior citizens are experiencing changes in their brains, and some of those changes are important for decision-making. Your loved one could be experiencing changes in the frontal cortex and they can sit and have tea or coffee and talk about sports, the news, or anything else—but yet, when it comes to their checkbook, they may not be able to understand things as well as they did in the past. They will not tell you they are forgetful and confused, but someone living with them may be able to identify the changes and may begin to take advantage of it.

These changes to the senior's brain help explain why someone that no one ever would have expected is giving money to the Canadian lottery or all these other scams. Ten years earlier, the senior would have said, "Are you kidding me? Of *course* it's a scam." But now, many things are believable to them because of changes in their brain.

If an unscrupulous caregiver is taking care of a person with Alzheimer's and says to this person, "You owe me $6,000 extra for this week because I did a lot of extra loads of laundry," that person might not appreciate that they are paying someone way more than what should be paid. It is even easier if the caregiver just fills out a check for $6,000 and puts it in front the senior to sign—they often will.

You need to be looking for red flags in your elderly loved one's behavior. One such red flag is that people with early-stage Alzheimer's may have difficulty with sequencing. They cannot remember which child was born first, second, or third. They can't remember what year they were married.

People in the early stages of Alzheimer's also can have more difficulty with short-term memory deficits than long-term. So they'll make an appointment and then call the office five times to verify the appointment. Each time they call, they will have no recollection of already having called.

Unfortunately, there is very little that the police can do to protect the vulnerable elderly until they are actually incapacitated. In cases where an elderly person is being financially exploited by a child, about all that can be done is to give the person a Mini-Mental Status Exam (MMSE) and try to prove the need for a guardianship. Then it is hoped that somebody more honest in the family can take over.

The law is not going to protect someone with capacity from making terrible mistakes. If a senior has legal capacity, they are free to make bad decisions.

Wolf in Sheep's Clothing

Vulnerable seniors are very susceptible to a wolf in sheep's clothing. Seniors are trusting and want to believe people. Money thieves can take advantage of this by presenting themselves as something they are not.

Real-Life Story: The War Hero from Church

A person who is supposedly a sophisticated developer and investor takes an 85-year-old man and his wife out for a fancy dinner. They trust him because he is a member of their church and, like the 85-year-old man, the investor is a veteran. In addition, he is supposedly a war hero.

He invites them over and drives them around his big apartment complex. He points out where he provides a free apartment for one of the church's ministers. He tells them that they will get a better-than-market return if they invest with him and his work for God's Kingdom. Oh, and by the way, he suggests that they get a reverse mortgage on their house, because that's free money, and he will help them invest that money to get a big "above market rate" return.

As it turned out, the couple lost $220,000, and the promissory notes were nonrecourse notes signed by the developer on behalf of illusory entities that he created. Not surprisingly, the provider of the investment product (the promissory note) was a non-registered entity. The lawyer for the couple filed suit using a consumer fraud statute.

Real-Life Story: The Wayward Priest

A local priest was going through the neighborhood surrounding his parish and offering Holy Communion to the homebound members of his church. On the surface, this seems like a typical activity that a priest might do for his congregation. However, this priest had a lawyer accompanying him. The pair would come into the homes of the sick or the old or those that couldn't make it to church for whatever reason, and the priest would perform a mass and offer them Holy Communion right in their living room.

After the priest was done, the lawyer would then offer his estate planning services to the homeowner. The homeowners, people too old and frail or too sick to attend church, trusted the lawyer, because he was accompanied by their priest.

It turned out that the beneficiary of the estate planning documents was none other than the priest. The priest owned properties in Florida and was hiding money in multiple locations. And naturally, the lawyer was receiving healthy kickbacks from the priest for his part of the exploitation.

Sadly, it is becoming more and more common to see cases involving trusted lawyers involved in the exploitation of the elderly. The exploitation almost always takes place through the drafting of legal documents—an area most people trust their attorney to properly handle. One of the fastest- growing scenarios involving lawyers requiring disciplinary action is lawyers who are exploiting elderly clients and taking advantage of their age and condition.

Fiduciary Relationship

A **fiduciary relationship** exists as a matter of law in certain relationships, such as lawyer-client and accountant-client. In certain other types of relationships, one party owes a higher duty to the other person than if it was a regular or non-fiduciary relationship. Typically, these relationships involve a fiduciary who is taking care of money or assets for the client. This is an important concept when dealing with financial exploitation.

If your loved one is being financially exploited, your elder law attorney may be able to show that the exploiter owed your loved one a fiduciary duty by establishing that a fiduciary relationship existed.

When determining if a fiduciary relationship exists, courts consider such factors as:

- the degree of kinship between the parties;
- disparity in age;
- disparity in health;
- disparity in mental conditions;
- disparity in education and/or business sophistication;
- the degree of trust placed in the dominant party; and
- the degree of dependence or reliance placed in the dominant party.

The idea that someone can create a fiduciary responsibility by disparity of knowledge and a whole host of other things is very important. If your lawyer can show, based on the facts and circumstances, that a fiduciary duty existed, the burden of proof shifts to the other side—to the fiduciary. That means instead of you having to prove your loved one was exploited; the money thieves must prove that they *didn't* exploit your loved one.

There is often a fiduciary relationship between home care workers and the person they take care of because of the degree of dominance and reliance and trust for somebody who is bathing a person, taking the person to the bathroom, and feeding the person. Once a fiduciary relationship is established, the defendant now bears the burden of proving that the transaction was objectively fair and reasonable and of benefit to the ward, or the transaction will be presumed invalid.

Creating a nontraditional fiduciary relationship is a great way to protect your loved one and to aggressively go after the money thieves. It can be a lifesaver when the elderly victim is in the early stages of dementia and is *vulnerable*, but not yet *incapacitated*. However, getting the your loved one to report the exploitation or go along with the prosecution of the exploiter is often a battle itself.

Seniors Tolerate Lesser of Two Evils

Seniors with dementia are more likely to put up with financial exploitation than report it. They know that they are being taken advantage of, but they don't want to turn in their abuser. They don't want their child or grandchild arrested, so they would rather just put up with it. Sometimes the relative exploiting them is the only person that can help them continue to stay in their own home. Maybe they don't drive anymore and they depend on that son or daughter to take them everywhere.

The worst part is that the child usually knows this and takes advantage of it. He or she thinks, "Well, it's going to be my money anyway; I'll just spend it now." They don't think the parents will live another 10 or 20 years anyway, so they don't worry about that. A lot of times, in this economy, maybe the children aren't even employed. They move into their parents' house and live off their parents' social security. Sometimes they will threaten the parents with putting them in a nursing home (although they'd never do that, since they are living off of their social security checks).

Oftentimes other family members will call the police and say, "I think my brother is taking advantage of my mom and I don't like it at all." More often than not, though, when the police talk to the mother, she says, "No, I want him to live here. I'm fine." Sometimes she will simply say, "I don't want to make things worse than what they already are." At that point, there is nothing the police can do.

Older people will often tolerate abuse because it is the lesser of two evils. That is probably the number one reason why abuse is never reported—the desire of the senior to stay at home is so great. Seniors are afraid that if someone takes their son, grandson, or whatever person out of the situation, now they will have to go to a nursing home. Given those two scenarios, they'll put up with the abuse so that they can continue to stay in their home.

Seniors who have been scammed by strangers don't want to tell their family because they are embarrassed, and also because they're afraid if they do tell the adult child, the adult child will say, "Dad, you can no longer care for yourself. We need to take you to look at other living options." Seniors know this is a euphemism for a nursing home.

It has been shown statistically that when a senior citizen has been a victim of crime, it can hasten their death. It is so disruptive to their life at a vulnerable time when trust is so important, that it often hastens their demise. Add the guilt of the grandson, or whoever was exploiting them, being put in jail, and the stress of moving to a nursing home—that's quite a lot of stressors.

Expert View: When the Indispensable Caregiver Is the Abuser

Linda Voirin, LSW, is the victims' advocate for the Seniors and Persons with Disabilities Unit, Office of Joseph H. McMahon, Kane County (Illinois) State's Attorney. The key point of this interview is the difficulty of prosecuting senior financial exploitation and elder abuse cases.

Q: Linda, you're not an attorney, but you've been a victims' advocate for over 10 years in the state's attorney's office, and you deal specifically with seniors and persons with disabilities. Describe the role of your team.

A: We have some attorneys specifically trained in dealing with the issues of abuse and the needs of the elderly, as well as attorneys who are trained specifically regarding the crimes that are committed against the elderly, such as financial exploitation. In addition, there is the concept of aggravated theft or aggravated assault. So as a victims' advocate, we are helping the elderly victim to understand, first of all, what's happening in the court system, being in communication with them as to court dates and what's happening in meetings with the attorney.

Often, if they have been victimized, it's a sign that there are other areas in their life that need looking into. Maybe they were particularly sought out as a victim because of a weakness or vulnerability that they had. Maybe they need extra care. So we try to assess their situation and then get them tied into services. We don't actually provide those services; rather, we make referrals.

Q: How often would you say that the person is victimized because, even though they're not technically incapacitated, they become vulnerable due to aging?

A: At least two thirds of the time. It's usually some vulnerability that's been identified by the abuser. Sometimes it's mental; sometimes it's physical. It can be as simple as the person no longer being able to do their banking by themselves and so they're asking others to do it. Maybe there is a vision loss and they are asking others to sign checks. These disabilities open the door for someone to be able to take advantage of them.

One of the biggest problems is that the abuser often is the person providing care to the older person. And the older person needs that help so much that they often tolerate the abuse. That is the number one reason why most abuse is never reported—because the senior's need for help is so great. For example, if you take away the son, grandson, or whoever who is assisting them in being able to stay at home, now they are in great fear that they are going to have to go to a nursing home—and often that's the truth. So when the senior reviews the two scenarios—stay at home and put up with the abuse, or don't put up with the abuse and go to a nursing home—they decide to put up with the abuse. It's the lesser of two evils.

An additional issue is the embarrassment and the shame. We see this on the witness stand. They admit that they didn't want to tell anybody that they have a problem, because if they tell their family members, they'll say, "Dad, you can no longer take care of yourself. We're going to need to look into other options" (go to a nursing home).

So that's an important piece to address before you can be serious about taking an abuser out of a home. When we go in and take the adult-child caregiver from a home and disrupt the senior's life, we have to know what kind of an impact that has. If the senior has to move to an assisted living facility, the lack of familiarity can be difficult to manage. It may be necessary; however, the elderly person might feel a sense of loss of independence.

Q: So it's a tradeoff that the abused person might not be eager to make, in spite of the abuse.

A: We have seen some difficult situations involving financial abuse. We recently had a person whose grandson was living in the basement. The elderly person never went downstairs because she physically could not handle the stairs. And the grandson was downstairs dealing drugs and doing drugs. But yet, he was the caregiver. Now that's a very dangerous situation on many levels for this elderly person. However, when we got involved, she was adamant, telling us that he was the only one able to keep her in her home. She was visually limited as well as physically limited. And we had to get a lot of care people to come in and come together to be able to begin a transition from that home. But if we had gone in and just ripped that guy out of the house and said, "That's the end of this!" prior to putting anything in place to assist with transitions, that would have been just devastating to her. It was devastating anyway, but it certainly would have been worse.

As you can imagine, after going through the traumatic experience of some form of abuse, the victim often feels lonely and depressed. If takes a lot of emotional and physical effort for the aged person to leave the comforts of their home and familiar surroundings and adapt to a new place. He or she will find the new environment strange and will miss the familiar. It may very well cause a decline, both physically and emotionally.

In addition, there is empirical evidence that when a senior has been a victim of a crime, it hastens their death. Just being a victim in and of itself is so disrupting at this vulnerable time in life when trust is so important.

The older person can't handle the stress—and on top of that, how are you going to get them to handle the guilt of putting a person who is close to them in jail? The same is true when it's not a family member but, rather, a caregiver who has been a person of trust for any length of time. The fact that that person is now no longer trustworthy and has turned on them and taken advantage of them in one way or another, this is a tremendous stressor. Often, we find caregivers who are stealing some of the medication and then there's that break in trust. It's a very difficult thing for someone to get over, and sometimes they don't get over it. And then they begin to question everyone, and now they say, "I don't know who I can trust, now I don't know if I can trust any caregiver or if I can begin to trust someone in a long-term care facility."

So it makes it extremely difficult to get people to testify against the ones who have betrayed their trust and financially abused them. And that's one of the reasons that so few elderly abuse cases are reported—and even the ones that are reported can be difficult to prosecute.

CHAPTER 11

CAREGIVING AT HOME? THE LAW REQUIRES A WRITTEN CONTRACT

People on the Alzheimer's care journey often progress through a trajectory as follows:

- memory loss ignored
- memory loss masked/denied
- unsafe alone
- aid needed, but fights back
- assisted living required
- nursing home required
- hospice care required/death

As your affected loved one's care needs increase, they will need a caregiver. This may start in the home and eventually they may need to move into a nursing home. That means there will be **personal-care agreements** and assisted-living facility or nursing home contracts to read, understand and sign. These documents seem harmless enough on their face, but they can be quite financially and personally dangerous. These documents can be constructive or destructive to both the loved one affected by Alzheimer's and to the family members who are either paid as caregivers or those who sign a contract they do not understand.

Millions of people are currently providing some level of in-home caregiving services for a loved one. Often times, providing those services is done at great personal cost and sacrifice. This chapter will focus on revealing the invisible obstacles you will want to avoid when dealing with a personal-care agreement among family members. We will also point out the hidden traps and dangers found in many standard nursing home contracts. Our hope is that these tips can minimize your personal cost and sacrifice and provide some peace of mind as your loved one's Alzheimer's trajectory progresses.

To-Do Checklist

❑ Know what you should be doing if you are providing in-care home to a loved one

❑ Get a powerful personal-care agreement drafted

❑ Understand the burden is on the caretaker and learn how to protect the caretaker (you, the reader!)

❑ Know when you need to pay employment taxes

❑ Understand the Medicaid issues and pitfalls with personal-care agreements

❑ Avoid the hidden traps of the nursing home contract

❑ Know your loved one's rights as a resident and protect them

The first stage of this journey, "memory loss ignored," is not easy to spot. The person affected, as well as their loved ones, may be dismissing the memory loss as part of the natural aging process. An individual in the early stages of Alzheimer's is often in good physical health, which makes it much easier to dismiss the occasional lapses in memory. The person feels good, looks good, and makes perfect sense most of the time.

Often seniors will either ignore their memory loss or will attempt to hide the behavior. In some cases, they are aware of their worsening condition but are afraid of being put in a nursing home.

When memory loss is first detected, this may be as suspicious as if you smelled "smoke in the kitchen." In many cases, their literally may be smoke in the kitchen because one of the most common dangers of memory loss is that the senior forgets and leaves a burner on or does not turn off the oven and eventually starts a fire in the kitchen.

Real-Life Story: Affected Loved Ones Are Often on a Similar Journey

A woman received a phone call from her grandmother asking her how to make spaghetti. The grandmother had been making spaghetti for more than 50 years, but now her memory was failing her in simple daily tasks. The woman visited her grandmother and was shocked to see the messy condition of the home and her grandmother's disheveled personal appearance.

Even more surprising was her grandfather's state of confusion. Clearly, both of them were in need of assistance, but neither one was willing to ask for help or give us control.

Once the memory loss has been detected by family or friends, the next stage is coming to the decision that the senior is "unsafe alone" and needs aid. It is not unusual for the senior to resist and fight to avoid assisted-living situations. While men seem to be more likely to fight back since control can be a bigger issue for a man facing Alzheimer's, it is not out of the norm for women to plant their feet and say, "I am not leaving my home."

On the Alzheimer's journey, the goal for many seniors and their families is to keep the seniors in their home (or in the home of an adult child) for as long as possible. This will necessitate the need for **in-home care**.

There are several hiring options when it comes to in-home care. The important thing to remember is that anyone hired directly usually creates an **employer-employee relationship**.

Most often, if an individual is being hired who will perform services and be under the direction and control of another, then an employer-employee relationship is created. This means you will have an employment tax issue to deal with. Many individuals ignore this at their own peril because they may prefer to pay cash to the caregiver.

There are many companies that specialize in in-home care. In these situations, the company is usually the employer of the caregivers that they provide. You pay the company and the company pays the caregiver. This is the simplest arrangement, since you do not have to do any bookkeeping, you don't need to worry about the employment laws, and/or tax reporting. You should still check to be sure that their caregivers are insured and bonded though.

Some companies that may appear to be employers of caregivers are actually in the business of merely placing freelance caregivers with families. These companies are being compensated through a finder's fee. Sometimes they take a portion of the caregivers' compensation. In this situation, the contract provided by this type of quasi-employment agency and in-home health- care provider clearly states that the company is not the employer of the caregiver. If you go this route, you may need a lawyer or CPA to make the determination as to whether or not you have become the employer and to then advise you on any next steps.

The majority of people do not have formal employer-employee contracts with their caregivers. Instead, most families prefer to handle these arrangements "under the table." Unfortunately, this often means that by the time people with no formal agreement call a lawyer, there are substantial issues of unpaid employment-related taxes, workers' compensation, and grossly inadequate bookkeeping.

If your loved one chooses to employ a family member, neighbor, friend, or freelance caregiver, they need to have a caregiver (employment) contract in place. We advise that you have an attorney draft or at least review the caregiver contract.

Real-Life Story: Read (and Understand) the Small Print

Read the in-home care contract carefully. When hiring in-home care, you need to understand the finer points of the contract. One family was surprised to discover that the in-home care provider whom they thought they were paying $18 an hour actually got paid time and a half on Saturday, double time on Sunday, and double time on holidays.

They were shocked when they got a bill of $72 an hour for eight hours of care on Sunday, the Fourth of July—four times the rate that they thought they had agreed upon!

Adult Children Providing Care

Situations in which adult children provide care for their elderly parents often start out as very casual arrangements. Many times, the first stage involves the adult children picking up some groceries for the parents while doing their own shopping or driving the parents to an appointment. Maybe they start giving their parents some money, or maybe they are coming over and cooking and cleaning and checking in on their elderly parents. You know, just being a good son/daughter. This all seems very normal and not in the least bit dangerous. Who wouldn't want to help out their mom or dad?

Then all of a sudden, a parent is diagnosed with Alzheimer's and the adult child has to quit his or her job or cut back their hours because taking care of the parent has become a full-time job. Most adult children aren't thinking that they need to have a lawyer draft a personal care contract, but that is exactly what needs to happen if they are providing care for their parents.

The elderly parent may well be writing checks to the caregiver child for gas, food, and time spent cleaning and doing laundry and the child may think they are keeping track of everything.

However, in all likelihood, everything is getting commingled and no one is keeping good records. The child is buying the parent's groceries and his or her own groceries and the child is paying some and the parent is paying some.

If the caregiver child is not keeping adequate records, they run the risk of being accused of elder abuse. On top of that, the senior receiving the care may end up being ineligible for Medicaid benefits. See Chapter 6 on Medicaid.

Sometimes the child will move in with the parents to better care for them and in other instances it is easier to have the parents move into the child's home. Often, in these situations, the child is appointed the **power of attorney for property** or at least the **power of attorney for health care** for the parent. In many cases, the parents add that child to their bank accounts so the child can pay bills for them, including reimbursements to the child.

163

Many states have passed legislation that has greatly expanded the definition of elder abuse. Family members who take on the role of caregiver may find themselves within the definition of people who have **heightened duties** relative to their loved one. Neglect of those duties can lead to both civil and criminal liability. A number of states have passed anti-elder-abuse power of attorney laws, which creates a presumption that if people who are **agents** are writing checks to themselves, that is presumed to be abuse of the **principal**, the parent. That means, the child will have to prove, hopefully by showing their caregiver contract to the court, that they are permitted to use the account to write checks to themselves for caring for their parent. A properly drafted personal-care agreement will refute accusations of elder abuse within the familial-care arrangement.

Legal Requirements of a Caregiver Contract

Each state will likely have different requirements for a caregiver contract. Proper and timely bookkeeping is almost always required—and unfortunately is the Achilles' heel of many of these contracts. Eventually the parents may need a higher level of care than their child can provide.

When one or both of them go to a nursing home and then apply for Medicaid, all those checks written by the child on the parents' account will be scrutinized and audited by the state.

If there was no personal-care contract in place between the parents and the child clearly describing the care to be provided and the compensation to be paid, many states will consider the transfers as non-allowable. A non-allowable transfer will create a penalty period of ineligibility for nursing home Medicaid benefits for the affected loved one. Some states have laws that say that care provided to a senior by a friend or family member is presumed to be "gratuitous." This can make it difficult in cases where a family member has been caring for a senior and not charging them and keeping adequate records. In those cases, the payments will be scrutinized.

The Real World

In a perfect world, people would approach an elder-law attorney before providing any care for their elderly parent who is suffering from Alzheimer's disease and give lawyers the opportunity to create a personal-care contract for them. Unfortunately, it is much more likely that people will wait and tell their lawyers that they have been caring for their mother for the last several months free of charge and now their mother's Alzheimer's is getting worse and they need to spend more time caring for her. Perhaps they need to cut back their hours at work. Whatever their situation, they have now realized that they need to have their mother pay them for the care.

While it is much easier to have an attorney draft the personal-care agreement prior to the start of the care, your lawyer can still draft the agreement after the care has started. The key is to demonstrate an increase or escalation in the care needs of the senior. In this case, the personal- care agreement can only be for services to be given after the date of that agreement.

Real-Life Story: Escalation of Care Required

A client walks into a lawyer's office and says, "I have been going over and taking care of my elderly mother for the past few months for a few hours a day. Now she's been diagnosed with Alzheimer's, and this is going to take up a lot more of my time and energy. I may need for her to move in with me and my husband, and I am going to need to start charging her. I want to set up a personal-care agreement for her."

In this situation it is not too late to create a valid personal-care agreement even though care has already been provided for free, because at this point the client is saying that the care needs have intensified and it's time for them to start being paid.

The key for Medicaid eligibility is that someone can never be compensated for care that was being provided gratuitously. For example, the parents lived with their son for two years and he did many things for them gratuitously, and then suddenly he says he wants to receive payment. He says that not only does he want to receive payment going forward; he wants to be compensated for all that previous care. That will be a big issue for Medicaid eligibility for the affected loved one, because a retroactive payment will be viewed as a gift and could create a substantial period of ineligibility for the person needing Medicaid.

The reality is that a lot of times people incrementally get into these situations. If people go to lawyers early in that process, lawyers would probably want to have them set up a low-level personal-care agreement. As the care increases, lawyers would increase the amount that clients are being paid proportionally to the number of hours they're working overtime. Lawyers need to have documentation in place to validate the changes of care level needed.

Personal-Care Agreements Tailored to the Family

There is no standard form for an interfamilial care agreement as it is not a one-size-fits-all situation. Unfortunately, simply pulling out a standard, generic employment agreement and changing the names will just not do in this situation.

Your lawyer should meet with the affected loved one and family to help create a personal-care plan that works for your loved one's situation. A personal care plan can be initiated by a telephone conference involving the affected loved one, the family, and the affected loved one's personal physician. A personal-care plan is the foundation upon which the personal-care agreement is built. It also provides written evidence of the health condition that necessitates and justifies in-home personal care. This is vitally important when defending payments being made between family members.

For people with Alzheimer's, the care plan recommendation will state that the caregiver is needed for health care, hygiene, welfare monitoring, nutritional management, and assistance with various activities of daily life. The recommendation will typically end with the statement that "without this care, the patient would require care in a nursing facility."

Most family members are not licensed health-care professionals. A licensed health-care professional, such as a medical doctor, physician's assistant, or other qualified individual, needs to be in charge of the case management and serve in an oversight capacity.

An alternative method of creating a care plan is to hire a licensed geriatric care manager to go to the person's house and do an assessment of the person's needs. The geriatric care manager is trained to do a survey of the physical environment within the home and an inventory of all resources available to the individual. After completing the assessment of the individual, the environment, and the resources, a personalized care plan is created. With the assessment in hand, your lawyer will be able to draft a customized personal-care agreement. The agreement should be tailored around what the care manager has identified as necessary care and other circumstances.

Personalizing the Care Contracts

You want the personal-care agreement to be customized as much as possible to make it a powerful document that will stand up to potential legal challenges. A generic contract that simply states that the elder is being provided care is just not going to stand up to the scrutiny of either the state's Medicaid department or the Department of Veterans Affairs. The affected loved one may need to qualify for public benefits; therefore, compliance with the complex regulations of the Medicaid department and Veterans Affairs must be taken into consideration.

Make sure your lawyer includes specific items to clearly demonstrate what activities of daily living are being provided. Personal-care agreements should incorporate the elder's answers to questions like, "What do you like to eat? What do you hate to eat? Would you like to rise early or sleep in? How often do you wish to have your hair done?" This level of personalizing the care contract can give a much more persuasive argument if the contract is later challenged.

You should include sample daily log sheets so that the caregiver can record activities on a daily basis. Consider hiring a bookkeeping and payroll service to handle the appropriate and timely employment and tax-return filings.

On occasion the affected loved one has an adult child who is a nurse, occupational therapist, or other licensed health-care professional who is legally qualified to provide more health care than a typical person. In those situations, it is important that your lawyer draft those health-care details into the agreement so as to provide a legal and contractual basis for a higher level of compensation than could be paid to a nonprofessional. The typical nonprofessional caregiver will be compensated based on the normal regional private-pay rate for a non-skilled in-home care provider. A professional may be compensated at a professional rate for performing a care service within that person's scope of expertise. It will always be necessary to keep proper records noting both the hours worked, as well as the type of care given during those hours.

In some cases, the adult-child caregivers need to move the affected loved one into their home. The caregiver may need to make some accommodations within their home for their elderly parent. If you are going to use funds from your loved one's accounts to pay for remodeling, then the remodeling must be documented as medically necessary. For example, adding a ramp for a wheel chair or making a bathroom more accessible are more likely than say upgrading your basement with a home theater. It is a good idea to check with your lawyer before undertaking an expensive remodeling project. A well written personal-care agreement should provide clear and simple written letters of instruction to the parties involved.

At some point after a personal-care contract has been created, the loved one receiving care will continue to decline as they move through the Alzheimer's care journey. Unfortunately, the majority of those individuals will exhaust their personal resources and be compelled to apply for nursing home Medicaid benefits. The Medicaid application process will include the state agency questioning the payments that were made to the caregiver.

If the personal-care agreement is not drafted correctly, or of proper records are not kept, your loved one could end up with costly penalty periods of ineligibility for Medicaid benefits during which they need to pay for care. Without appropriate evidence, like written logs of daily caregiving services, a caregiver could be accused of being an elder abuser.

Burden on Caretaker

Personal-care agreements are important for the person receiving the care, but they are also important for the caregivers.

Individuals that take on long-term-care duties often see a decrease in earning potential and frequently have to cut into their own savings to provide for the person they are caring for. Caregivers usually cannot afford to quit their nine-to-five job, but they may be forced to cut back their hours in order to care for an elderly parent. These caregivers often put their own retirement at risk to care for a parent.

A recent national survey of caregivers showed that over half of the responding caregivers reported a medium to high level of burden. Another national survey of the full-time workforce also came to the conclusion that individuals who were employed full time and who also had caregiving responsibilities suffered from lower well-being than non-caregivers.

Caregiving can have detrimental health and psychosocial conse- quences for caregivers. People frequently hear stories of the healthy wife who is taking care of her husband who is suffering from dementia. Often, when the husband finally passes, the wife's health takes a quick downturn and she passes soon after. Being a caregiver, especially for a loved one, takes a toll.

Because of this burden, don't be afraid to seek out the family lawyer (or the lawyer in the family) and ask them to create personal-care contracts that specify that you, the caregiver, will agree to help the elderly person for a set amount of time in exchange for an hourly wage for these services.

After the death of the affected loved one, lack of a personal-care agreement often leads to an estate administration problem. Many states provide a legal basis for an uncompensated caregiver to file a claim against the estate. Creditors of the deceased (with lawful claims) generally will be ahead of the beneficiary when it comes to collecting on a claim. If the family caregiver does not have a personal-care contract, the caregiver will have a hard time establishing his or her status as a creditor with an allowed claim. In fact, many states will stop caregivers in their tracks if they do not have a written contract. Even if caregivers are able to imply an oral contract existed, they are faced with presumption that their services were rendered gratuitously. It is possible to still prove that your services were not gratuitous, but it is much easier to do with a written contract.

Employment Taxes

Did you know that the Internal Revenue Service has special rules that apply specifically to workers (caregivers) who perform in-home services for elderly or disabled individuals? Most people are not aware of these rules. Because caregivers generally work in the homes of the elderly or disabled individuals and these individuals have the right to tell the care- givers what needs to be done, caregivers are usually treated as employees of the individual for whom they provide services.

If you are a caregiver employee for a family member, the employer (family member) may not be responsible for employment taxes. (Warning: Reread the first sentence of this paragraph. It *does not* say that you as the employee are exempt from paying income taxes. Rather, it states in a much more limited way that the affected loved one is not responsible for your portion of employment taxes.) However, the affected loved one (employer) still needs to report the caregiver's compensation on a W-2. (See Publication 926 Household Employers Tax Guide for information.)

If it is determined that caregivers are not employees, the caregiver is still required to report compensation as income on Form 1040. Depending on the facts and circumstances, the nonemployee caregiver may have to pay self-employment tax. Under a personal care agreement, family caregivers do not owe self-employment tax on the payment for a family member unless they are in the business of providing care to others.

The Invisible Opponents: The Backstory of Cultural Tradition, Judicial Bias, Elder Abuse Statutes, and the State Medicaid Department

Generally, when you provide a service for someone else you can expect to be compensated. However, when the same services are performed by a family member, the presumption is that the services were performed for "Love and Affection." In other words, they are presumed to have been performed for free/gratuitously. This can be quite a presumption to overcome, because the prejudice against contracts among relatives dates back to the 1800s, when it was assumed that relatives performed services for the mutual convenience of everyone in their household. Not only do you need to overcome these legal presumptions against familial contracts, there are also deep-rooted cultural beliefs about caregiving among family members.

For example, there are strong cultural beliefs at play that suggest parents should receive reciprocal free care from their children because of the years they spend as uncompensated caregivers raising their children.

Your personal-care agreement needs to clearly state that the transfers made under this contract are not for love and affection, but rather they are for services rendered to the elder by the caretaker for fair market value.

Fair Market Value

The first thing a hearing officer or judge is going to check when evaluating a personal-care agreement is whether the caregiver is being paid fair market value for his or her services.

This is especially the case when the services are being performed by a family member. As we know, services performed by relatives are often presumed to be gratuitous. However, that doesn't mean that relatives and family members cannot legitimately be paid for the care they provide.

Medicaid applicants are generally required to show that the funds transferred to the related caregiver and the services received were exchanged for fair market value.

So what exactly is fair market value? Fair market value is an estimate of the value of an asset, if sold at the prevailing price at the time it was actually transferred.

While that may sound simple enough, determining the prevailing price of eldercare services is not as easy as it sounds. Just about everyone, including hearing officers and judges, has a different opinion as to how to determine how much caregivers should be paid. The authors always include two or three fee quotations from commercial in-home caregiving companies in their personal care agreement binder. Nonetheless, there is no formula to determine a fair market hourly wage or even who should make that determination

After establishing the fair market rate, you still may face questions about what services are included and, in the case of Alzheimer's disease, how wages would change with intensified care responsibilities as the disease progresses.

Expert View: 10 Tips for Caregivers

Jo Huey is nationally known as an author and trainer of those who provide care for people with Alzheimer's disease. One of her most memorable experiences was evacuating more than 30 New Orleans memory-care residents when Hurricane Katrina came to town. She and some of her staff spent the next two and a half months in temporary housing. All the residents had a diagnosis of Alzheimer's disease or some other type of dementia—individuals who typically would stay in an assisted-living facility until the end of their lives. Jo became affectionately known to her staff as "Hurricane Huey."

"We were required to do hurricane drills every year," she says, "but after the drill, you're actually able to go *back* to the residences that you evacuated. After Hurricane Katrina, we had nothing to go back to—and that leads to dealing with the difficult ambiguities of what to do next in the midst of a disaster." She has served as a nursing home administrator in Colorado and an assisted-living director in Louisiana.

Q: If you had a magic wand as you think of the years you've been dealing with persons with Alzheimer's, including your own mother, what would you love to have people know about working with people with Alzheimer's and their families?

A: It's important to understand the complexity of what happens and to be able to look at the whole family situation.

People can present themselves so well—even a person with Alzheimer's. Often they are very angry at a family member, but many times that is the family member who is helping them the most. Once mom or dad is upset with the most caring family member, then other family members get involved and suddenly sibling rivalry is ignited and any other historic family issues and that have been simmering for a long time add fuel to the fire.

So both other family members and professionals can easily get sucked into the middle of all of these family issues that are going on. . . . One of the most important things is making sure that the older person is able to make their own decisions, and that often gets overlooked. When families go to war with each other, the senior's wishes can be lost in the battles.

Q: Can you help us to sort out this issue of the person with dementia who is actually angry at the family member who is trying to help them the most? Because it really is quite common that people come in to our (the author's offices) complaining about all the grievous and horrible things that some family member is doing to them, or taking their stuff. What's really going on there?

A: Very often it's just their fear of losing their things. They know something is really wrong with them, but if they let go of their things, then somebody will take advantage of them. That's one of the ways this disease presents itself. People are trying so hard just to hang on. And anyone that seems to disturb that, then that person becomes the most suspect. The target of their anger, of course, are the ones that are present and helping them the most and are the ones who end up being accused of causing many of the bad things that are happening. The person with Alzheimer's no longer has the capacity to sort out complicated cause-and-effect.

For some reason, we just get angrier at the people who are closest to us. We get paranoid that somebody is hurting us when, in reality, they're doing everything they can to help.

Q: How do you think family members and professionals could be alerted to the fact that it can be relatively common for an older person to falsely accuse a younger person of theft or manipulation?

A: I've seen some professionals conduct family meetings in their office, and I believe that is the right strategy. You get everyone together and spend time just getting acquainted and then you can pick up on what's really happening by watching the body language of everyone in the room. Body language can be much more informative than just listening to their words. After the family meeting, have the people separate and then talk to each one about the same things. When interviewing the client, ask questions like, "Tell me what you need your money for. What are you going to do with it? What are your plans? Who do you want to have money and things after you're gone? Why?" This type of interview will help the attorney sort out whether or not their client still has the ability to appreciate what they have and what is really happening around them.

I think the professional needs to be very calm during these meetings. The professional can provide great value to the client and family, because most families seldom get around to having those types of discussions.

If you look at the model of a geriatric care manager, one of the first things they do is go to the home and interview the individual who needs care and also the family. They do this before they work on the care plan. If other people would consider the model of the geriatric care manager, they would get the family together and do an assessment before making a decision on the right course of action. Too often, I've seen situations where the senior and their attorney, for example, "charges the enemy" before really knowing who is a hostile and who is a friend.

Q: Is it very common for people to go through the full Alzheimer's disease trajectory and then actually die of Alzheimer's?

A: Although Alzheimer's disease is an illness that ends in death, most often people die from other causes first, such as stroke or heart attack. The most common death for people with Alzheimer's or a related disorder is infections, especially pneumonia and sepsis (an infection that goes into the bloodstream).

The most common forms of sepsis for people with Alzheimer's tend to be from things the ordinary person wouldn't even think of, mainly urinary tract infection, also called UTI, or a bowel backup. The tough reality is that it's very difficult for a person with Alzheimer's to tell you what's going on internally and it tends to get overlooked by the care staff because the behaviors of somebody with a urinary tract infection often are not seen as an infection. They get very ill very quickly and it happens so fast.

Q: When I [author Rick L. Law] first met you, you shared with me some principles to improve communication with someone affected by Alzheimer's disease. What do we need to know?

A: The name of my book is *Alzheimer's Disease, Help and Hope: Ten Simple Solutions for Caregivers*. The 10 Absolutes are communication tools to allow caregivers to know what to say and what not to say when working with people affected by Alzheimer's. My goal is to help people motivate those with Alzheimer's to do the right things, such as taking a bath. I also want to help people to avoid the nonstop battles and enjoy what time they have together. There are still lots of things that a person with Alzheimer's may be able to do, and they still need to have some meaning and purpose in their lives. Too often, everything is taken away from them and they feel like there is nothing left worth living for.

The Ten Absolutes are

- Never argue; instead, agree.
- Never reason; instead, divert.

- Never embarrass; instead, distract.
- Never lecture; instead, reassure.
- Never say, "Remember"; instead, reminisce.
- Never say, "I told you"; instead, repeat/regroup.
- Never say, "You can't"; instead, do what they can.
- Never command/demand; instead, ask/model.
- Never condescend; instead, encourage/praise.
- Never force; instead, reinforce.

Expert View: The Marriage of Technology and Alzheimer's Caregiving—Staying Safely at Home Longer

The Oaks, a United Methodist Continuous Care Retirement Community is located in Orangeburg, a little inland from Charleston, South Carolina. What attracted us was the exciting work being done there to give people diagnosed with dementia the ability to live at home with dignity while providing peace of mind for family members and caregivers. The Oaks provides traditional senior services and care combined with looking to the future, recognizing that there is extraordinary pressure to move long-term care from the institutional facility back into the community.

The visionary leader of the Oaks is the Rev. James McGee, CEO. When we met with him and Stacie Pierce, the director of the technology/caregiving solution program called Live at Home Technologies, they had recently returned from meeting with IT wizards in Israel. The purpose of the trip was to further their research, development, and implementation of innovative technologies to provide remote in-home care for people affected by dementia. Some of the activities monitored include motion of an individual or lack of motion, bed and chair activities, medication access, patterns of movement through the home, daily body weight, daily blood pressure and blood glucose, time spent in the bathroom, the opening and closing of interior and exterior doors, and appliance usage. Stacie answered a few questions we had.

Q: Tell me about how technology is helping seniors to live at home longer.

A: This is something I'm passionate about. I'm a caregiver first and foremost. We take care of people, and we use technology to enhance that care so that when they're not safe anymore, then they understand what their other choices are.

There are more than 70 million baby boomers about to hit the market. We need to have choices available. When you talk about Alzheimer's, it's an epidemic, and people are living longer and the disease is being diagnosed earlier. Technology gives people more living options.

We help people live at home with the support of honest and reliable family members who live nearby. One family lives 90 minutes from our facility. The daughter-in-law and son-in-law live about 500 yards away from the two disabled family members. The father has Alzheimer's and his daughter, who lives with him, is 62, and she's developmentally delayed and has an IQ equivalent to a three- or four-year-old. The wife recently died of a massive heart attack, most likely due to caregiver fatigue. This woman was taking care of her husband with Alzheimer's and her disabled 62-year-old daughter. So now you have a family who is asking, "What can we do?" The man was born in this house and the daughter was raised there. They have been a part of each other's lives for 62 years, and they have their patterns. If we separate them, she'll go to an institution and he'll go to assisted living or a nursing home, and they'll both probably die much sooner.

We examined their living patterns. We worked with the family to figure out what the rules will be. He still likes to go out and get the mail. They live on a busy road, so we put a door sensor on the door. Then I started thinking, if he leaves the door open, how am I going to know if he came back in? So I put a floor mat down on the inside. So if he opens the door and there's no pressure on the floor sensor within 20 minutes, then I know he didn't come back in. We've had that system in place for three years now. Anytime an alert is sent out, it goes to one of the other family members who live nearby.

The daughter had a history of falling in the bathtub. So we established a rule that if there's pressure on a mat in the bathroom for more than 30 minutes, then an alert is sent to one of the family members. We can set it up so that an alert goes to one of the family members, on their cell phone or their computer, and then they can connect to the house, turn on the camera inside, and actually view to see if someone is on the floor. We here at the Oaks do not have access to the cameras—only family members do.

You can't have technology without some sort of caregivers, as well. Nonetheless, the technology can make the caregiver's life more livable. Otherwise there's a much higher likelihood that the caregiver will die before the person being cared for.

I met with a man yesterday who's in his mid-80s and still an active businessman. His wife has Alzheimer's and he needs help with care. He says, "I still enjoy my work. I have to go out of town to do business. I can't take care of my wife 24/7." He wants to have a solution so his wife can continue to live at home and to provide the family with some sanity at the same time. We can put in a system that will allow him to go out and play poker and still keep his wife safe by providing alerts to him or other caregivers.

Most people don't even know that these types of solutions are available. I have been certified as an assistive technology practitioner and an aging-in-place specialist. This type of training allows us to work with homebuilders and remodelers to design appropriate systems within residences.

Q: Let me introduce you to Scott Ewing, chief operating officer at the Oaks. The Oaks is providing caregiver monitoring for his 87-year-old mother who still lives at home 600 miles from Orangeburg. Without the technology in her home, she would need to live at an assisted-living facility. Scott, how does this technology help your mother?

A: I'm a nursing home administrator so I understand costs very well. I had to have a discussion with my family about the risks versus reward of keeping Mom at home. My fear is not that she falls, because I know she's going to fall—she's elderly—but if she falls and something happens and she's undiscovered, that would be terrible. But with this technology, we can know that if she falls we'll get an alert. My mother is a retired schoolteacher and not particularly affluent. The cost of a nursing home where she lives in Maryland is $7,000-plus a month. Assisted living would be $5,000-plus a month.

When you put in the technology, you have up-front costs for the system—but that is less than one month of assisted living. With what we have put in, my mother can continue to live in her home of 53 years, and all her neighbors are around to help and support her. If I get an alert, I call a next-door neighbor and they'll check on her. She's had some of the same neighbors all her life. It's been tremendous and very liberating for her to have the technology so she can stay at home.

(While we were doing this interview, Scott got an alert that his mother had been in the bathroom more than one hour. He excused himself and went to make a call. He returned and told us that she had responded somewhat sheepishly, "I'm sorry, son, I must have fallen asleep.")

CONCLUSION

Expert View: The Hope of Vanquishing Alzheimer's Disease

Harry Johns is president and CEO of the Alzheimer's Association.

Q: Let's start with a common misperception: Alzheimer's is not a fatal disease.

A: Most people still do not realize the basics of Alzheimer's. Alzheimer's disease is progressive, degenerative, and ultimately fatal. Unfortunately, people still think of the disease as "a little bit of memory loss." I talk to people all over the country. Many times, when I say that Alzheimer's disease is progressive, degenerative, and fatal, people respond, "Alzheimer's disease isn't fatal!" Well-educated people in high positions will argue back at me, "You don't die of Alzheimer's disease!"

Q: Do you often see denial when early symptoms appear?

A: Denial is a really powerful evolutionary protection. If we simply accept all the terrible things that go on in the world every day and don't operate on some level of denial, we would all cease to function. Denial helps us to deal with everyday life. Unfortunately, denial as related to Alzheimer's disease leads to many bad outcomes.

Q: What are the earliest signs of Alzheimer's?

A: Memory loss is often the first sign that others recognize and attribute to Alzheimer's disease. Here are the 10 early signs and symptoms of Alzheimer's, as identified by the Alzheimer's Association:

1. memory loss that disrupts daily life
2. challenges in planning or solving problems

3. difficulty completing familiar tasks at home, at work, or at leisure

4. confusion with time or place

5. trouble understanding visual images and object spacing

6. new problems with words in speaking or reading

7. misplacing things and losing the ability to retrace steps

8. decreased or poor judgment

9. withdrawal from work or social activities

10. changes in mood and personality

Q: Does it always start with memory loss?

A: There really is a general lack of knowledge throughout our society about the progression of this fatal disease. Most people believe that Alzheimer's disease always starts with memory loss, but it doesn't. My mom had the disease. The first thing that she admitted to was not being able to balance her checkbook. All through her life, every week she had balanced her checkbook to the penny. She just could not do it anymore. That is what is called the loss of "executive function."

Q: What is the family doctor's role in all of this?

A: I want people to know that medical doctors just do not want to give their patients the diagnosis of Alzheimer's disease. That means that you are encountering people in their workplace, community, and home who have not been diagnosed by their physicians as having dementia, but they are definitely cognitively impaired.

In fairness to the doctors, there are those on the positive side of the bell curve who are doing exactly the right thing. Unfortunately, most doctors do not want to give the diagnosis because it is terrible. They do not want to be the one who tells the individual or the person's family that their loved one has a diagnosis of an incurable disease.

The medical profession faced a similar situation in the 1960s. Back then, there were really no effective cures for cancer. Based on numerous studies at the time, more than 90 percent of all doctors admitted that they did not tell a patient with cancer that they had cancer. Today, we are in the same situation with Alzheimer's disease. The drugs that we have available to treat those with Alzheimer's disease do not work well enough to cure the disease. In addition, they don't work long enough for sufficient numbers of people for doctors to feel that they have an effective tool to aid their patients. Nonetheless, it is important that people do get diagnosed early, because the drugs that we do have now work sufficiently well for some people to substantially lengthen and improve their functional lives.

Returning to the issues of the early signs of Alzheimer's disease, memory loss is the most frequent first sign recognized by the family as a sign of dementia, but there are other changes too. Behavioral changes often occur first. People may either withdraw from others or they may become more aggressive. Look for personality differences in a person as a possible sign of the beginnings of Alzheimer's disease. The problem is compounded by the fact that many people affected by Alzheimer's recognize the changes within themselves and then actively work to hide what is going on from others.

Q: What resources are available to patients and families?

A: The Alzheimer's Association has resources that can help people to know more about how to deal with Alzheimer's disease. More information is available at www.alz.org. There is a helpline available 24 hours a day, 365 days a year, at (800) 272-3900. The people who answer the phones are highly trained social workers, so they know how to counsel others about the disease. In addition, the Alzheimer's Association website has a host of resources available to everyone.

The Alzheimer's Association has a program called Trial Match, which is set up for matching people to clinical trials that are very specific to a person's circumstances, locale, and the availability of the trials, and also the kind of care they're already getting. The Alzheimer's Association is available to help by telephone, and there are many great volunteers in local chapters that can help individuals or their family members.

The Alzheimer's Association offers various intervention programs that can make a difference in a person's functional life.

Many of these intervention programs provide as much assistance to people as what some of the drugs can do. We have programs that help caregivers, as well as programs that help individuals who have this disease stay engaged—the kinds of things that keep them active, the kinds of things that don't have them withdraw in the way they otherwise would. We know from the science that if people stay engaged and don't withdraw as much and do those kinds of things, it can improve their functional lives on a comparable level to what some of the drugs can do.

Q: What are your hopes for the future?

A: The future for the Alzheimer's Association would be that Alzheimer's disease is vanquished and we are out of business in just a few years. But, most likely, we will continue to exist, because there will be a need for additional research, and a continual evolution of the types of drugs that will be available. There will be a need for guidance to assist patients and families on the pathway of care. Modern medicine has conquered many diseases, and we can certainly hope that the same happens with Alzheimer's disease. That would be the ideal.

GLOSSARY

A

Acute care condition: a diagnosis that you can get well from. Medicare generally covers acute care conditions. The opposite of chronic care.

Advance directives: written documents such as the living will, power of attorney for health care, power of attorney for property and the do not resuscitate order (DNR) that set forth health decisions to be made once the person can no longer make these decisions for him/herself.

Advocate: a person chosen to act as a decision maker for the person with Alzheimer's. This should be someone who can look a medical professional in the eye and insist that certain wishes be carried out.

Agent: the person being granted authority in an advanced directive/power of attorney is the agent. This person is also referred to as the *attorney in fact*.

Alzheimer's disease: a degenerative brain disease of undetermined cause that is the most common form of dementia, usually starting in late middle age or in old age, that results in memory loss, impaired thinking, disorientation, and changes in personality and mood. The Alzheimer's Association labels the disease as degenerative, progressive, and fatal.

Alzheimer's journey: individuals with Alzheimer's often progress through this trajectory:

- Memory loss ignored
- Memory loss masked/denied
- Unsafe alone
- Aid needed
- Assisted living required

- Nursing home required
- Hospice care required/death

The **family of a loved one with Alzheimer's** often progresses through a **complementary trajectory** which may have some of these components:

- Memory loss ignored
- Memory loss masked/denied/facilitated
- Memory loss assistance needed by loved one, but hidden from "outsiders"

Arbitration clause: one of the methods used by nursing home attorneys to cut nursing home losses from litigation is to include binding arbitration clauses within the standard form contract. Nursing homes are raising arbitration clauses as a defense, even within the context of wrongful death actions and personal injury suits.

Assisted living facility: nursing home or other type of facility for people who cannot live alone because they have chronic care conditions, such as Alzheimer's disease.

B

Beneficiary: one for whose benefit a trust is created.

C

Capacity: generally defined as the mental ability to perceive and appreciate relevant facts and make rational decisions.

Capacity worksheet: a checklist of sorts aimed at helping attorneys to be able to assess their clients and determine whether or not the client has diminished capacity.

Care managers: licensed clinical professionals, usually with advanced degrees, with extensive knowledge of health care, aging, and different issues that affect people with disabilities. They are often nurses, social workers, and licensed clinical counselors.

Caregiver child: child taking care of a parent with diminished capacity.

Charitable pooled trust or **d4C trust:** an irrevocable gift that provides both a lifetime income from premium investment options and an unprecedented charitable tax deduction.

Chronic care conditions: a condition, such as Alzheimer's disease, that is not going to improve. The opposite of acute care.

Cognitive impairments: mental impairments associated with confusion, forgetfulness, and other memory issues.

Community spouse: for purposes of this book, the term "community spouse," as defined by nursing home Medicaid regulations, is a spouse who continues to live in their personal residence within the community while married to a person who has been institutionalized in a nursing home.

Community Spouse Resource Allowance (CSRA): exempt assets that the healthy community spouse is allowed to keep when one spouse has a disease like Alzheimer's and needs Medicaid assistance. The federal government allows the states to choose levels of exempt assets within a range of what's allowed under the federal standards. This will be the amount of money available to a community spouse as a resource allowance when an institutionalized spouse applies for benefits under the Medicaid program. Most states require you to fully disclose all assets owned either jointly or individually by either spouse.

Conservator: another term for guardian. Typically handles financial affairs while the guardian handles personal/health-care needs. Some states use the terms "guardian" and "conservator" interchangeably, while some states use the term "guardian" to refer to a guardian of the person and "conservator" to apply to a guardian of the estate.

Contractual capacity: level of capacity required for the execution of inter-vivo trusts, deeds and non-durable powers of attorney. Contractual capacity is defined as the ability to comprehend and understand the terms and effect of the contract.

Countable assets: assets that count towards the state determined max' mum for Medicaid purposes. These include bank accounts, certificates deposits, money market accounts, stocks, mutual funds, bonds, retirem accounts, pensions, second cars, second or vacation homes, and any (items that can be valued and turned into cash.

Custodial care: assistance with preparing meals, bathing, grooming, toileting, and other activities of normal-daily life. Medicaid may pay for custodial care. Rules vary per state.

D

d4A or self-settled trust: a special needs trust funded with property belonging to the beneficiary and/or beneficiary's spouse, such as a direct inheritance, recovery in a personal injury lawsuit, or a gift.

d4B or Miller trust: a trust in which a person has assigned his/her right to receive social security and pension payments, in order to avoid having too much income to qualify for benefits like Medicaid.

d4C trust or **charitable pooled trust:** an irrevocable gift that provides both a lifetime income from premium investment options and an unprecedented charitable tax deduction.

Dementia: a form of mental disorder resulting from degeneration of the brain. For purposes of this book, dementia includes degeneration of the brain caused by Alzheimer's disease, Parkinson's disease, and as many as seventy other causes. Dementia does not refer to traumatic brain injury.

"Death is imminent": in medical terms, a determination made by the attending physician according to accepted medical standards that death will occur in a relatively short period of time, even if life sustaining treatment is initiated or continued. The "relatively short period of time" is defined as six months. One becomes qualified for hospice if death is imminent.

ᵖendency and Indemnity Compensation (DIC) Benefits: unmarried ˢes, dependent children, and parents of veterans can all potentially be ˹ for the wide variety of VA benefits.

ᵈ **capacity:** a partial or complete reduction in a person's ability ᵘnicate, to comprehend and assess information, and to make ᵒns.

When drafting estate planning documents such as a ᵗ, one option is to offer the client a disability panel ᶠ sufficient incapacity to trigger the removal of the ᶦncludes both family members and one attending physician. They often empower a majority to rule in the decision making, but some clients may be more comfortable with a unanimous decision.

Disabled: a person is disabled, for purposes of this book, if unable to manage his or her person or estate due to mental deterioration or physical incapacity.

Do not resuscitate (DNR) order: instructs health care professionals not to perform cardiopulmonary resuscitation if a person's heart stops or if he or she stops breathing. DNRs are signed by a doctor and put in the individual's medical chart. The DNR is the only advance directive that is also a doctor's order or a physician's order for medical care.

Durable power of attorney: a power of attorney that continues in effect after the principal becomes incapacitated and is unable to supervise and direct the agent. *See also* **power of attorney.**

E

Early-onset Alzheimer's: the appearance of Alzheimer's symptoms beginning before the age of 65. This is rare, making up around 5% of all Alzheimer's cases.

Employer-employee relationship: is a relationship that has employment tax implications. This comes up in caregiver contract situations. If an individual is being hired who will perform services and be under the direction and control of another, then an employer-employee relationship is created.

Exempt: for purposes of this book, "exempt" is used primarily to mean assets of an individual which are not counted towards the determination of eligibility for means-tested public benefits.

Exempt assets: assets that do not count against the beneficiary for **Medicaid** eligibility purposes, such as the following:

- the principal place of residence, subject to restrictions
- household and personal belongings
- one car
- burial plot/prepaid funeral plan
- cash value of permanent life insurance policies up to $1,500

- a small amount of cash (this varies from state to state, but typically a single Medicaid applicant may keep about $2,000 while married couples who both require Medicaid may keep a higher amount)

F

Fiduciary relationship: a legal relationship of trust. These exist as a matter of law in certain relationships, such as between lawyer and client. However, a fiduciary relationship can also be found as a matter of fact. Courts consider such factors as:

- the degree of kinship between the parties;
- disparity in age;
- disparity in health;
- disparity in mental conditions;
- disparity in education and/or business sophistication;
- the degree of trust placed in the dominant party;
- the degree of dependence or reliance placed in the dominant party.

Once you have a fiduciary duty by fact patterns, you can argue undue influence in a financial exploitation situation. This is important because you can shift the burden of which party must prove, or disprove the exploitation.

"15-minute reset": a way to detect memory issues such as dementia. Often, persons with excellent social skills (still common in women in their 80s and 90s) are able to hold a conversation that includes all the correct words and head nods. However, somewhere around 13 or 14 minutes they will start the conversation over again, almost as if they were playing a tape.

Financial exploitation: the act of taking advantage of a person suffering from dementia for financial gain. Financial exploitation is overwhelmingly committed by persons related to the victim or in a position of trust.

Five-year look-back period: after application is made for Medicaid benefits, the state agency will look at all gifts/transfers made in the last five years. Gifts/transfers may not be made simply to be eligible for Medicaid benefits. The burden of proof is on you to prove that the gifts/transfers were *not* improper.

Forensic accounting: a specialty practice area of accounting that applies accounting techniques to solve legal issues. Often used to investigate and document financial fraud.

Fraudulent conveyance: a transfer of property that is made to swindle, hinder, or delay a creditor, or to put such property beyond his or her reach.

G

Geriatric care manager: a person with special training in the area of elder care. For purposes of a personal care agreement they are trained to conduct a survey of the physical environment within the home and an inventory of all resources available to the individual.

Guardianship: a legal relationship that is established and monitored by state courts under state laws. It is a mechanism for empowering someone (the guardian) to act on behalf of an incapacitated individual (the ward) with a legal disability—for purposes of this book, Alzheimer's disease.

Guardian ad litem: often referred to as "the eyes and ears of the court." Before the temporary guardianship hearing is held, the court appoints a guardian ad litem to visit the alleged disabled person and make a determination and report back to the court as to whether emergency relief is necessary and reasonable under the circumstances.

Guardian of the estate: person responsible for the care, management and investment of the estate. In some states, a guardian of the estate is referred to as a conservatorship and may do the following for the ward:

- make financial decisions;
- enter into contracts;
- estate planning;
- file lawsuits;
- sell real estate;
- apply for government benefits.

Guardian of the person: assists the ward in the development of maximum self-reliance and independence and may:

- make medical decisions;

- oversee the residential placement of their ward (with court approval);
- ensure that the ward receives proper professional services;
- release medical records and information.

Grantor: a person who makes a transfer of property by deed or writing.

H

Heightened duties: a heightened duty of care means that more care is expected than in a situation with a normal duty of care. Family members who take on the role of caregiver may find themselves within the definition of people who have heightened duties relative to their loved one.

Hospice care: a team approach to caring for an individual in his/her final stages of a terminal illness, such as Alzheimer's. The goal of hospice care is to provide comfort, reassurance and support for the dying patient and their family and friends.

Hospital insurance: *see* Medicare coverage.

Housebound: a term used, for purposes of this book, in veterans' benefits. People are considered housebound if they have a permanent and total disability and either have additional disability estimated at 60% or more, or are substantially confined to their residence or the immediate premises due to a disability that is reasonably certain to remain throughout their lifetime.

I

Improved Pension: also known as, Special Monthly Pension, Aid and Attendance, or Non-Service Connected Pension: a Veteran benefit

Incapacity: refers to someone who is not mentally fit or able to safely handle their own decision-making. "Capacity" generally means the mental ability to perceive and appreciate relevant facts, to understand the consequences of those facts, and to make rational decisions. "Incapacity," then, describes the lack of those abilities.

Incompetent: lacking capacity to make decisions for one's self. *See also* **Incapacity**.

In-home care: care that takes place in the affected one's home.

In-patient: a key term for Medicare eligibility. Medicare helps pay for in-patient care in the hospital or skilled nursing facilities following a hospital stay. The patient must be "admitted" and not merely "under observation." Typically requires a 72-hour hospital stay.

Institutionalized spouse: as defined by nursing home Medicaid regulations, an individual who:

- requires care in a medical institution such as a nursing home; and
- is married to a spouse who resides in the community at least one day of the month.

Inter vivos trust: a trust that becomes effective during the lifetime of the trustmaker/settlor/grantor and provides access to the trust corpus according to the terms of the trust. Often called a living trust or revocable living trust.

Irrevocable asset protection trust: a type of trust that as a general rule, cannot be revoked or changed after it has been signed; or a revocable trust that by its design becomes irrevocable after the trustmaker dies.

L

Legal disability: for purposes of this book, Alzheimer's disease or another form of dementia.

Life-sustaining treatment: any medical treatment, procedure or intervention that in the judgment of the attending physician, when applied to a patient with a qualifying condition, would not be effective to remove the qualifying condition or would serve only to prolong the dying process. Those procedures can include, but are not limited to, assisted ventilation, renal dialysis, surgical procedures, blood transfusions and the administration of drugs, antibiotics and artificial nutrition and hydration.

Limited guardian: a guardian who has been appointed by the court to exercise the legal rights and powers specifically designated by court order entered after the court has found that the ward lacks the capacity to do some, but not all, of the tasks necessary to care for his or her person or property, or after the person has voluntarily petitioned for appointment of a limited guardian. A limited guardian is appointed by taking away certain rights of an individual and giving certain rights.

Living will: a document (advance directive) that only takes effect when two doctors certify in writing the creator of the living will is irreversibly ill or critically injured and near death.

Look-back period: *see* Five-year look-back period.

M

"Means-tested": a descriptor indicating that a benefit, such as Medicaid, is available only if someone qualifies for certain poverty limitations.

Medicaid: a program typically administered by the individual states, with funding from both the federal government and individual states. Medicaid is a means-tested health care benefit program. To have medical expenses paid, applicants typically must meet impoverishment guidelines, which include both income and asset limitations.

Medicaid Compliant Annuity (MCA): an asset-preservation and income-enhancement strategy that was originally put into the federal law to permit single individuals and married couples to have a better financial outcome. The bottom line is that money that would have had to have been consumed as an available asset will be transformed into an allowable income stream.

Medicaid trusts: a term used to describe a trust created for the purpose of protecting assets from being treated as available for spend down on health care services. The grantor/trustmaker makes a gift of their assets to the trust with the express purpose of qualifying for Medicaid. The history of Medicaid trusts has been a continual assault by federal and state governments to eliminate the ability of individuals to use trusts as asset protection devices while qualifying for nursing home Medicaid benefits.

Medicare: a non-means-tested federal health-care program that provides benefits primarily to U.S. citizens who are over 65, blind, and/or permanently disabled. Medicare was not created to pay for 100% of an individual's health-care expenses. For those individuals who are over 65, blind, and/or permanently disabled, and also have insufficient income and assets to pay deductibles, it is possible to be "dual eligible" for both Medicare and Medicaid. Medicare is supposed to pay for acute care, assuming the person needing the care is placed as an in-patient.

Medicare coverage: hospital insurance, medical insurance, Medicare advantage plans, and Medicare prescription drug plans, all with their own eligibility requirements.

Hospital Insurance (Part A): Most people age 65 or older who are citizens or permanent residents of the United States are eligible for free Medicare hospital insurance.

Part A helps pay for inpatient care in a hospital or skilled nursing facility (following a hospital stay), some home health care and hospice care.

Medical Insurance (Part B): Anyone who is eligible for free Medicare hospital insurance (Part A) can enroll in Medicare medical insurance (Part B) by paying a monthly premium. Individuals that are not eligible for free hospital insurance, can buy medical insurance, without having to buy hospital insurance, if you are age 65 or older and you are:

- a U.S. citizen; or
- a lawfully admitted noncitizen who has lived in the United States for at least five years.

Part B helps pay for doctors' services and many other medical services and supplies that are not covered by hospital insurance.

Medicare Advantage Plans (Part C): Individuals that have Medicare Parts A and B can join a Medicare Advantage plan. Medicare Advantage plans are offered by private companies and approved by Medicare. Medicare Advantage plans generally cover many of the same benefits that a Medigap policy would cover, such as extra days in the hospital after you have used the number of days that Medicare covers.

Part C plans are available in many areas. People with Medicare Parts A and B can choose to receive all of their health care services through one of these provider organizations under Part C.

Medicare Prescription Drug Plans (Part D): Anyone who has Medicare hospital insurance (Part A), medical insurance (Part B) or a Medicare Advantage plan (Part C) is eligible for prescription drug coverage (Part D). Joining a Medicare prescription drug plan is voluntary, and requires an additional monthly premium for the coverage. Some beneficiaries with higher incomes will pay a higher monthly Part D premium.

Part D helps pay for medications doctors prescribe for treatment.

Medicare Supplement/Medigap policies: Medicare supplement insurance fills the "gaps" between Medicare benefits and what a person must pay out-of-pocket for deductibles, coinsurance, and copayments. These policies pay only for services that Medicare deems as medically necessary, and payments are generally based on the Medicare-approved charge. Some plans offer benefits that Medicare does not, such as emergency care while in a foreign country.

Mental incapacity: an absence of mental capacity in which one is unable to properly control one's assets and/or one's healthcare decision making.

Mini-mental state exam (MMSE): commonly used test to detect memory issues. It can be used by clinicians to help diagnose dementia and to assess its progression and severity.

Minimum monthly marital needs allowance (MMMNA): the amount of monthly income that the state Medicaid agency calculates the community spouse needs to survive. This varies from state to state.

N

Non-allowable transfers: (Medicaid) Gifts can be classified as "**non-allowable transfers**" if made during the five years preceding a Medicaid nursing home application, the transfers would be lumped-together as a total and a penalty assessed—and that penalty will not start to run until the senior-Medicaid-applicant is "otherwise eligible," which means not until she has completed her spend-down. Then the penalty period will begin, and she won't get benefits until it ends. In many states, 100% of what the state characterizes as a gift must be repaid by the recipients to cure a penalty which denies nursing home Medicaid coverage.

O

Orientation questions: simple questions to see if the individual can understand the time and the place they are in, who they are, and what's going on currently in the world.

P

Personal care agreement: for purposes of this book, an agreement in which a person contracts to care for an individual with dementia. It is critical to affirmatively state within the agreement that the transfers made under the contract are not for love and affection, but rather they are for services rendered to the elder by the caretaker for fair market value.

Plenary guardianships: a person who has been appointed by the court to exercise all delegable legal rights and powers of the ward after the court has found that the ward lacks the capacity to perform all of the tasks necessary to care for his or her person or property. This is the main type of guardianships and consists of guardians of the person and guardians of the estate.

Power of attorney: documents that allows a family member or trusted friend to have legal authority to carry out the wishes of the person suffering from Alzheimer's once they are no longer able to speak or act for their self. They can be for (i) financial matters or health care decisions or for (ii) property.

Parties to **power of attorney:** the person granting the authority by signing the documents is referred to as the principle and the person being granted the authority is the agent or attorney of fact. This person stands in for the principal and is authorized to take almost any action for the principal so long as that action is included in the powers of attorney document.

A "**durable**" power of attorney continues in effect after the principal becomes incapacitated and is unable to supervise and direct the agent.

Power of attorney for financial decision-making: a power of attorney limited to financial decisions.

Power of attorney for health care: a power of attorney limited to health-care decisions.

Power of attorney for property: a power of attorney limited to property decisions.

Pay down: *see* spend down.

Physician Orders for Life-Sustaining Treatment (POLST) programs: provide a platform for end-of-life conversations between doctors and patients and a uniform way to document the wishes regarding those decisions so the patient's desires are understood and properly prioritized.

Q

Qualifying conditions (living will): the conditions that trigger a living will to come into effect. They typically trigger a doctor to speak to a family member about making an end-of-life decision, or cause an attending physician to say no to more life treatment or to make a referral to hospice.

R

Rebuttable presumption: a presumption that is made by an overseeing authority (e.g., that gifts that a person made were made to impoverish oneself to qualify for Medicaid) that must be rebutted, or disproved, or it will be taken as a true statement. The Medicaid rules in most states create a rebuttable presumption that all gifts given by seniors to their family members were done for the sole purpose of impoverishing themselves so as to be able to qualify for nursing home Medicaid. You can rebut that presumption with evidence. The evidence needs to be done at the time of the gift. This is made much more difficult once a person has Alzheimer's disease or other dementia to be able to prove the reason that money was transferred between family members.

Respite care program: programs that offer substitute caregivers and are designed to provide temporary relief for the primary caregiver from day-to-day responsibilities. Some respite programs are offered by paid health aides, while others involve volunteers from churches or other groups

Responsible party: for purposes of a nursing home contract, signing as a responsible party means you are assuming liability for any debts created by the resident. Under the Federal Nursing Home Reform Act, nursing homes are not allowed to include "responsible party" language in their contracts anymore, but the term is almost always included anyway.

Revocable trust: a type of trust that can be revoked or changed at any time.

S

Short-term guardian: a guardian appointed to take over the guardian's duties, each time the guardian is unavailable or unable to carry out those duties. A short-term guardian may be appointed in writing, without court approval.

Skilled care: care of a certain level. Usually, patients needing skilled care need a higher level of care than normal, generally from a certified or licensed nurse or health-care professional. This level of care is lower than long-term care.

Skilled rehabilitation center: a center where one can receive a level of skilled care.

Snapshot date: the date used to calculate a couple's countable assets for Medicaid eligibility purposes. Typically, this is the date that the spouse enters a hospital or nursing home for a continuous stay of at least 30 days.

Spend down/Spend down requirement: a situation wherein a person must first use excess assets (as defined by Medicaid regulations) to privately pay for medical bills, prior to becoming eligible for nursing home Medicaid coverage.

Springing power of attorney: a power of attorney that does not take effect until the principal becomes incapacitated.

Substituted judgment: refers to the preferences of the ward that were "previously expressed" (i.e., before the ward became incompetent).

Successor agent: term used for agents next in line behind the primary agent, usually used when dealing with advance directives. If the primary agent is not available, a successor agent may be called upon.

Surrogate decision maker: a court appointed decision-maker for incapacitated person, generally authorized to make health care decisions for the patient. This is not a guardian.

Sustenance: as referred to in this book, feeding tube and hydration for a person being cared for under the terms of an advance directive; if you note that you want sustenance on an advance directive, you are actually *requiring* the use of a feeding tube and hydration.

T

Temporary guardian: a guardian who has all of the powers and duties of a guardian of the person or of the estate which are specifically enumerated by court order. There are certain circumstances (including a guardian's death, incapacity, or resignation) in which the court may appoint a temporary guardian. For a temporary guardian to be appointed, it must be deemed necessary for the immediate welfare and protection of the alleged disabled person or his or her estate on such notice and subject to such conditions as the court may prescribe.

Testamentary capacity: the ability of a person to understand or recognize the following elements in relation to each other (also defined as of being of sound mind and memory):

- the nature of the act of making a will
- the nature and extent of their property
- those persons who are the natural objects of their bounty
- the disposition of their property according to their own plan

Testamentary trust: a legal and fiduciary relationship created through explicit instructions in a deceased's will. A testamentary trust goes into effect upon an individual's death and is commonly used when someone wants to leave assets to a beneficiary but wishes to control the time, place, and manner of the distribution. Testamentary trusts are typically irrevocable.

Testamentary will: a legal document that is used to transfer the probate estate to beneficiaries after the death of the testator.

Trust: a legal document that transfers title of property from one person, the trust maker or settlor, to the beneficiary.

V

Vulnerability: there is no legal standard for vulnerability, but vulnerable individuals are more likely to make poor financial decisions and are prime targets for scam artists and criminals.

W

Ward: the subject of the guardianship; sometimes referred to as the conservatee.

Will: *see* Testamentary will.

Wrongful resuscitation: the act of resuscitating a person against their wishes. These wishes are usually detailed in their advance directive.

ABOUT THE AUTHORS

Kerry Peck

Mr. Peck is the managing partner of the Chicago law firm Peck Ritchey, LLC. He is past president of the 22,000-lawyer Chicago Bar Association. His clients include families, hospitals, banks, the State of Illinois, County of Cook, and City of Chicago. Mr. Peck was retained by the City of Chicago Department of Aging to rewrite the State of Illinois Elder Abuse and Neglect Act, and co-authored the book Alzheimer's and the Law, published by the American Bar Association. Mr. Peck has also written articles for the Chicago Daily Law Bulletin, Chicago Bar Association Record, Illinois State Bar Journal, and various other Bar Association journals and newspapers. He frequently teaches attorneys and healthcare professionals across the country.

Mr. Peck has been repeatedly selected by his peers in statewide surveys of Illinois attorneys as a "Super Lawyer," an attorney to whom other attorneys would refer their family. He was also named a member of the Leading Lawyers Network. In 2014 Kerry Peck was honored with the Justice John Paul Stevens Award, the Chicago Bar Association's highest honor. The Stevens Award recognizes lawyers and judges who have demonstrated outstanding character and commitment to community throughout their careers.

Mr. Peck has extensive experience in advising individuals and banks charged with the administration of estates and trusts, and guiding fiduciaries through the probate process, including appearing in court; assisting in the transfer of assets and resolution of claims; and the implementation of decedent's estate plans. He vigorously represents all parties in will contests and contested guardianships, including minors and disabled adults. In addition, Mr. Peck assists families with planning for disabled children or other family members who are, or are likely to become, disabled and require special protection.

Rick L. Law

Mr. Law is the founder and lead attorney of Law Elder Law, LLP, located in the Chicago metropolitan area. The law firm motto is, "We help you keep more of what you have!"

He has focused in his practice on the issues of retirement and aging. He is a nationally recognized authority in the areas of estate planning, asset protection, income tax efficient retirement, and nursing home Medicaid benefits.

For many years, he has been named the number one elder law estate planning attorney in Illinois by *Leading Lawyers Magazine*. In recognition of his numerous published articles and his books focused on retirement and long-term care issues, he was selected as an official member of the *Forbes Finance Council*.

He has been quoted in Wall Street Journal, AARP Magazine, TheStreet .com, and numerous professional publications. He is a co-author of two additional books, *Alzheimer's and the Law: Counseling Clients with Dementia and Their Families* and *Cruising through Retirement: Avoiding the Potholes*. Mr. Law is both an engaging author and a dynamic speaker.

When he is not working, writing, or speaking, he loves to be home at his farm with his wife, Rose, his adult children, grandchildren and his horses.

Contact Mr. Law at www.lawelderlaw.com